HOW TO DELIVER A SONG WITH IMPACTFUL EMOTION

A Ministers 40 Year Collection of Winning Recipes to Revolutionize Your Singing Experience

by Grammy Award Winning Songwriter,
Producer, *and Vocal Coach*

ROBERT "ELIJAH STORM" DANIELS

HOW TO DELIVER A SONG WITH IMPACTFUL EMOTION

A Minister's 40-Year Collection of Winning Recipes
to Revolutionize Your Singing Experience

By
ROBERT "ELIJAH STORM" DANIELS

Edited by Rosetta Daniels
Printed in the United States of America

By
ABM Publications
A division of Andrew Bills Ministries Inc.
PO Box 6811, Orange, CA 92863

ISBN: 978-1-931820-90-5

All rights reserved solely by the author. The author guarantees all contents are original and do not infringe upon the legal rights of any other person or work. No part of this book may be reproduced in any form without the permission of the author. All scripture quotations, unless otherwise indicated are taken from the King James Version of the Bible, Public Domain. Scripture taken from the New Kings James Version. Copyright 1982 by Thomas Nelson. Used by Permission. All rights reserved.

For information and permissions, contact BIGG KIDD MUSIC by email at supernatualvocals@gmail.com, by phone 440-941-1779 or visit www.SupernaturalVocals.com for more information.

Tags: Robert Daniels / Non-Fiction / Music / Singing / Music Industry / Religion / Christianity / Teaching / Vocals / Vocal Mechanics / Lessons / Vocal Lessons / Emotions / Self-esteem / Ministry / Entertainment Industry / Education / Community / Students

Dedication

First, I want to dedicate this book to my Father God in Heaven, Who is Lord of my life, eternally, and Whom without His grace, and the gift of salvation through His Son Jesus Christ, I would not be here to share this gift.

To the loving memory of my beautiful mother, Hallie Marie Green, who kindled my love for music in first introducing me to singing and playing the piano. I love you mother, and I miss you. I know you are in paradise singing and dancing with the angels.

To the loving memory of my father in the music business, Mr. Norman Whitfield, who poured so much into me, and gave me the opportunity to live my dreams. Thank you Whit. I will do my best to continue to pour into others like you poured into me.

TABLE OF CONTENTS

	Acknowledgements	7
	Testimonials	11
1	The Fundamentals	15
2	Voice Strengthening & Singing Correctly	31
3	Developing A Listening Ear	35
4	Song Interpretation & Delivery	43
5	How To Nail An Audition & Live Recording	51
6	The Attitude of An Impactful Singer	69
7	The Anointed Vessel	75
8	Inside Look At My Studio History With…	95
	Special Thanks	101
	About The Author	103
	Ministry Information	105

Acknowledgements

First and foremost I thank you God for preserving my life and giving me purpose. I depend on you daily and I thank you for Your Precious Son Christ Jesus in Whom I am redeemed!

I want to thank my beautiful wife Rose...sweetheart, God has blessed me with more than I could have asked for, or even imagined with you. I could not have written this book without your support and I am grateful for your love and faithfulness. You are truly a priceless gem and the Proverbs 31 wife!

To Mrs. Bey, thank you for your love, support, and being such an amazing mother. We all love you very much! I am forever grateful for all you and Mr. Bey have poured into me.

I thank my children and grandchildren for a legacy fulfilled. I love you all so much more than you could ever know.

I thank my family which is an arsenal of sisters, brothers, aunts, uncles, cousins, nieces and nephews who always give your love and support. I love you and let's keep singing!

Thank you to my students, colleagues, friends, and professionals who I've learned so much from as well.

Thank you to my cousins Chris Powell and Raymond Swearingen, my best friends DC Calip and Thomas Dawson, Jamie Jones, Eric Jackson, Emanuel Officer, Steve Clemons, Stacey Piersa, Sam Watters, and once again I do not want to get into any trouble because God has truly blessed me people in my life who love me in word and action!

Mrs. Gina Holcomb, thank you for impacting my wife's life in such an amazing way, and for your magnificent review!

I want to give a special thank you and acknowledgement to my brothers and sisters and spiritual coverings in the faith that have encouraged me, prayed and fasted for me and with me, and have ministered to me with love and acceptance in this season of my life for which I am humbled and grateful:

Apostle Dr. Andrew Bills, thank you for blessing my wife and myself with favor and for supporting us in our Abraham move to Ohio. I've always wanted to write a book and here we are. God is so good! You and Pastor Ann Marie are such a blessing to our lives.

To my precious Pastor Frank and First Lady Cassandra Starks, there is not enough room on this page to express how very precious and valuable you are to our family. Your constant love, acceptance, guidance, encouragement, intercession, support, and impartation is priceless, and I love you both very much!

To my good friend and brother Pastor Kenneth Mulkey, I thank you for your love, support, friendship, accountability, teachings, and encouragement. You and your wife Angel are such an inspiration to our family. God bless you!

To my cousin and Pastor Arlyn Davis, I thank you for taking me in and giving me the opportunity to grow and be used in my God-given gifts and passion. You and First Lady LaKeysha are an amazing couple in Christ.

To "Auntie" and Uncle, thank you...for everything!

To my little sister Minister Katrina McCrary and family...well, you know how much you are loved and cherished as a true sister and friend, prayer warrior, and anointed woman of God. God has given us a such a blessing in you and your family, Apostle Ty and all. We love you!

To Pastor Bennie and Angela Mosley and family, we love you and thank you for friendship, prayers, and encouragement.

Apostle Dr. Kazumba and Glory Charles, thank you for your love, friendship, support, encouragement, and understanding the ministry God has given to me and my wife! We love you and your precious family.

To all of our friends at the YMCA, S.T.A.R.S. and Solich Music, thank you for partnering with us upon our journey from California to Ohio!

God bless everyone who has been a blessings to our lives, and to whom we are a blessing to, in Jesus name. Amen.

Testimonials

"This is a great recipe book. It includes all of the right ingredients for developing your talent and staying true to oneself. God, talent, humility, discipline, work ethic, all will guide you to connect and deliver to an audience."

Storm masterfully connects scripture into everyday practice of singing techniques with emotion and expression. It really helps the performer visualize the desired emotion of a lyric or song they are trying to achieve and give them the confidence to go for it. You feel scripture, you feel a song.

I love this quote from the book, *"That's a good way to redirect nervousness, anxiety, and overcome fear, by understanding your assignment and going in once again like a special task force agent to complete the mission."* There is no better feeling than when you walk away from an audition knowing you emptied, exhaled it all on the stage.

Storm poses a simple question, Why do we sing? It seems simple but knowing your WHY is critical for having an emotional impact on your performance and audience.

This book is a great guide for any singer who struggles to connect with a song, an audience, or themselves. Singing encompasses your entire body and soul and you have to be willing to commit fully. After reading the scripture inserts, I found myself asking, Do I fully commit to my faith, marriage, life, performance each time, every time, every day?

I would love for Storm to come and work with my young singers at my school. His passion is evident and contagious. His connection with people is genuine and real and I know they would walk away with great information to improve their performance.

Listening is one of the most important aspects of singing. Most singers do not spend enough time on this skill. Storm presents some great ways of breaking down the skill of listening that is useful in all parts of your life.

After teaching music for 30 years, this was an insightful reminder of why I do what I do! Thank you for the many healthy reminders of all of the aspects of delivering an emotional, stop them in their tracks performance! BRAVO!"

+ Gina Hersek Holcomb, Music/Vocal Teacher and Show Choir/Band Director
Mayfair Music Department, Bellflower Unified

Testimonials

Dear Reader,

My best friend, who is more like my brother, Robert "Storm" Daniels, is an extraordinary songwriter and producer. He truly has a God-given gift for music that can't be measured. We met over 23 years ago, when I finished playing NBA basketball for the Lakers, and he offered to take me to one of his recording sessions. I was blown away watching him work, and developed an instant passion for music that has been with me to this day.

He is an amazing vocal coach and teacher, as he shares with you many of his incredible techniques in his new book, "HOW TO DELIVER A SONG WITH IMPACTFUL EMOTION." He covers things like breathing, posture, warming up your vocals, and other things that one may not even consider, that will help to transform your singing to the next level.

Please treat yourself to this amazing book, and take your singing career to the next level, and really learn how to deliver a song.

+ Demetrius "DC" Calip, Former NBA Player,
Basketball Coach and CEO of The Gymbrats LLC
http://www.thegymbrats.com
http://thegymbrats.blogspot.com

"Proverbs 18:16 reads, a man's gift maketh room for him, and bringeth him before great men. I am so glad to see God opening the doors for Robert Daniels, while witnessing the man of God's gifts making room for him, in his career, and in the blessings for his family."

"HOW TO DELIVER A SONG WITH IMPACTFUL EMOTION is an encouragement to help anyone, as it will inspire you to strive for your dreams. This book will compel you to keep trying; to not give up, no matter what your gift is! Robert's testimony in what God has revealed to him over the years in the music business is invaluable because it imparts hope into you to let you know that if he can make it, the very same God can and will do the same for you. All those things he has experienced in his life thus far, have all come together working for God's purpose. In the midst of all the amazing instruction in this book, Robert speaks about everyone having a purpose from God to fulfill, and gives insight based on the Word of God in how to accomplish walking in your purpose from God, as you glorify Him with the gift(s) He's given you.

Robert has helped our praise team from Heirs International Ministries do amazing things vocally and he taught us how to blend our voices together when worshipping in song. Since reading his book, I have applied some of the breathing techniques he shares and noticed how it improved my delivery instantly. Once can never stop learning how to be better and we are very proud of what God is doing with the Daniels family. Robert is blessed with an amazing wife in Rose, and is continuing to perform miracles in their lives. This book is a must read, and will give hope in some way to those who read it."

+ Dr.'s Frank and Cassandra Starks,
Owners of In Him Global Media and
Founders of Rekindling the Flame of Romance Marriage Ministry
www.KCWGTheTruth.com
www.RekindlingtheFlameofRomance.com

CHAPTER 1

The Fundamentals:
Breathing, Posture, Pitch and Tone

> *The Fundamentals*
>
> 3 Through wisdom a house is built,
> And by understanding it is established;
> 4 By knowledge the rooms are filled
> With all precious and pleasant riches.
> 5 A wise man *is* strong,
> Yes, a man of knowledge increases strength;
> 6 For by wise counsel you will wage your own war,
> And in a multitude of counselors there is safety.
> + *Proverbs 24:3-6*

Q: What is the first lesson you teach a new student?

A: Well, the first thing I do is evaluate my students as we establish a rapport, and see what kind of background they've come from in music and what inspires them to sing. I ask questions like, *"Are there other people in your family that sing or do music (mother, father, sibling, etc.)? What does music do for you? How does music affect you? What do you want to accomplish through your music?"*

Some of my students have goals that are not career goals so singing for them may just be a hobby. Some of my students may want to improve their worship experience in their choir. Other students of mine may want to receive breathing exercises to build their lung capacity for sports or just for a better quality of life. I had one of my students take my class to help them run a marathon. Some of my students who major in music also want to be educated in vocals and understand how the mechanics work to apply them to a performance. I also teach actors and actresses who are particularly interested in connecting more emotionally when singing as well as improving their vocal prowess. And then I have some students who genuinely enjoy singing and it is therapeutic for them, so they continue to improve as they go, as with any other commitment.

I then find out what my students strengths and weaknesses are, pull from my own experiences, and then apply methods for how I can help them, and impact their lives. Then I teach my students how to impact other lives with their voice. I help them with what I have, finding out the mechanics of their vocals, and even imparting the Word of God as a foundation to build from in confidence, in developing instinct and execution relative to how everything works together when using their vocal instrument. You really do use your entire vessel to deliver and you, like many people, will discover this as you develop your emotional connection at the deepest level. So I will help you identify your purpose for singing, and impact those who come into contact with your gift. What that impact looks like may vary but the impact will be undeniable.

Fundamentals: Learning to Sing

The process of learning to sing is not something that is usually accomplished in a matter of months. It is a very slow process that entails proper posture, breathing and diction. But one of the most important aspects of singing is learning how to listen.

Posture

It is always best to sing in a standing position with your feet planted firmly on the floor, approximately 12 inches apart from one another, with one foot slightly ahead of the other. While reaching your arms as high above your head as you can, slowly let your arms fall back to your sides as this will contribute to your relaxed stance. Your back and chest should have a nice comfortable balance in positioning. A substantial amount of your weight should be placed on the front portion of your feet to allow greater flexibility in breathing, and also to create a more energetic impression when singing in front of an audience. Your knees should be slightly bent, to allow you to stand as firmly as possible. Never lock your knees while singing as doing so can weaken your stance.

Good posture can be defined as a stance achieved that allows for an aligned spine (no twisting). This provides for good voice production so a secure stance is definitely to a singers advantage. The positioning of your head, hands, arms, chest, back, abdomen, feet and knees all play a vital role in improving your voice quality. A proper singing posture will enhance your breathing, optimizing your breaths, which will result in a better sounding voice for you. Ok, let's continue...

Your shoulders should be positioned down and back firmly, without tension or droopiness. Once again, your arms should hang at your sides in a very relaxed manner, slightly bent at the elbows. Place your fingertips firmly on the sides of your thighs and try your best to keep them there (for the time being as it is important to remember the fundamental stance before venturing off into choreography on any kind). Your head position should be determined by the focus of your eyes which should be straight ahead. Your neck should be relaxed all the way around, which will ensure that your head is neither too far back nor too far forward. You should not be twisting your neck when singing as this may strain your neck muscles which will suspend your voice box. Your chin should be parallel to the floor.

You have different stances. Your stance (feet) should not expand past your shoulder width. You can also put a foot forward (about a head forward) keeping your chin forward and relaxed. Don't put your chin down. Be relaxed because putting your chin down brings tension, and tension brings problems.

Your abdomen should be flat, firm, and held in an expandable position. Place one hand on your abdomen while breathing to ensure your abdomen is relaxed and expandable. <u>Breathing from your diaphragm (lower abdomen) should expand when you inhale</u>. Once again, a proper singing posture will enhance breathing so no slouching! When you slouch, your tummy can't expand fully to optimize your intake of oxygen which is extremely important for quality, power, and control.

TIPS: *Good singing posture...*

#1 Standing in front of a full length mirror will help you gauge your overall posture and appearance.

#2 Standing placing your heels, calves, buttocks, shoulders, and back of your head against a wall is a good place to start from when gauging your posture.

#3 Your standing posture should be firm yet create enough fluidity as if you were standing on water.

HOW TO DELIVER A SONG WITH IMPACTFUL EMOTION

MY OPERA COACH was at least 80 years old. I remember thinking when I first began working with him as a child, that he had a very **powerful voice**. So when I first came to my opera coach, he actually had me **standing up singing**. In order for me to do the vocal exercises he gave me, I had to stand up, because it was then that I found out that I didn't have any power.

He taught me how to throw my voice and sing loud enough to fill a room with a 26 piece orchestra. It's important to stand when you want to project with power. There are certain limitations you experience when sitting. But after 8 or 9 months, I was able to sit and maintain that power. However, my timbrel changed. My tonality and the sound of my voice changed. I then found out that I loved sitting when recording. But of course it all really depends on the song and what you need to deliver.

If it is a song that will take a lot out of me emotionally and vocally where I have to deliver power, then I cannot sit, I have to stand. But if it's a ballad and I'm relaxed, then I am able to sit on a stool at a mic something like Tammie Terrell and Marvin Gaye used to do. It really depends on the person, the music, and the delivery. Most singers will sing and deliver in a standing position which I recommend best. Standing up is best for delivery. When standing you are more in attack mode. You can sway side to side or even pull something out of the air. You've gotta reach and pull from a place of emotion. Pull it down, reach out and take it.

My mentor, Norman Whitfield, I don't believe ever allowed anyone to sit down when singing. Standing gives you more in singing power than you have when sitting.

Sitting Posture

When singing while sitting, sit in a relaxed state to eradicate tension. When singing, tension happens a lot, especially when you are anticipating the difficulty of delivery. Don't "think high" but instead, just hit the note. Don't reach, just get there through the natural process.

Practice opening your mouth, breathing, and exercising your lungs. When a patient has a surgery in the hospital, sometimes the doctor has them blow into an apparatus to strengthen their lung capacity. You will have to use your diaphragm to inhale air and release air very slowly. Try to do this for a full 60 seconds or as long as you can. Inhale, and then exhale. Take all day, as long as you can, as many times as you can when doing this.

Don't overdo it though so you don't get dizzy or black out! You will start to yarn and get a little sleepy. While inhaling you'll fill up your diaphragm and your tummy. Breathing properly means your tummy pushes out when you inhale and retracts in when you exhale. Be mindful NOT to tense up in your throat. Relaxation is so very important. You can breathe rounding your mouth like an oval, and then you will feel your breathing affect your upper head and throat. Don't contract and tense up because it limits your power and causes stiffness which doesn't feel or sound good.

Breathing

Breathing efficiently when you sing is a combination of great posture and skillful inhaling and exhaling. Good posture allows you to get a deep, full singing breath. If you slouch, or you're too rigid, your diaphragm locks and prevents you from getting a correct breath for singing. The diaphragm holds all your power...depending on what style you are singing. Also, in general we want to minimize vibrato because it takes up too much air.

As you work through your breathing exercises, place one hand on your chest and the other hand on your abs, then after doing so, place one hand on your chest and one hand at your side. Then place one hand on your abdomen and at your side before returning both arms back at your sides. As you inhale, use your hand to feel whether your chest remains steady. It should stay in the same position for inhalation and exhalation. If your chest rises during inhalation, you will create tension in your chest and neck. You will feel your other hand moving out with your abs and sides as you inhale and back in toward your body as you exhale.

Breathing to sing works a little different from your normal breathing patterns when speaking. Knowing the keys to proper breathing will allow you to use your breath to make specific types of sounds and carry them out longer. Your proper breathing technique will really come into play when you have to deliver a song with attack. You will practice inhaling to sing in breathing by opening your body, breathing slowly and steadily, and catching a quick breath. You will practice exhaling to sing- breathing by blowing in the wind, recognizing resistance, and suspending the breath. Breathing to sing comes more easily when you are posturing yourself properly to accompany your breathing.

Breathing is so important for control, power, and ability to relax. When you breathe, air passes through when you take in breath and push out. I can never over stress breathing. You can fill up on breath standing still, in a shoulder stance, or while relaxed. Be still, and stand, without tension.

A key technique in execution is how you position your larynx. Your larynx consists of muscle, cartilage, and bone in your neck, and the more you are able to be still, the more friction and pressure you'll alleviate. Your vocal chords are like elastic rubber bands so the lower in range you go, the more they contract, and the higher in range you go, the more they thin out.

Also, exercising is so important for stamina and regular exercise will greatly improve your breathing.

Warming Up Your Vocal Chords Introducing Scales

When warming up your vocal chords, I love to introduce the scales. I start low, usually below middle C near G. I take bass singers and tenors even lower depending on their initial range. Then we begin the process of stretching the vocal chords at the appropriate pace. I go over this technique with repetition, especially for beginners, because I want them to feel the sensation of the scale.

(For examples of Warm Up Exercises, please visit www.supernaturalvocals.com in the tutorial section to see the exercises there)

Some scales are the hum, the mum, the ee's and the ah's.
Ee, ee, ee, ee, ee, ee, ee, ee, ee (4x)
Mum mum mum mum mum mum mum mum mum (4x)
Ah ah ah ah ah ah ah ah (4x)

A slower pace when executing the scales is more challenging because it requires more controlled breathing, and more breaths. A faster pace of executing the scales is easier to accomplish because it has quicker breaths and it is easier to grab your breaths when you need them to keep the fluidity of the scale. Pay attention to your diaphragm and how you breathe, and how your air passes through your diaphragm, chest, and throat and when singing in falsetto where you can develop your head voice.

Be relaxed during this journey. Being tense takes away from your energy output, and you need all the stamina and reserved energy you can get when you are delivering a song with impactful emotion! You want to experience the impact as your audience does and it takes work, so don't go adding to it by being tense. Who wants to experience a tense situation? Most likely not your audience unless you are performing in a drama or horror film, ok so you get my point, right? Laughter is good for breaking tension, so you may want to develop a sense of humor if you don't have one already, ok? Moving on...

HOW TO DELIVER A SONG WITH IMPACTFUL EMOTION

The larynx opens and closes as we go up the scale. Traveling all the way up the scales, sing each vowel (listed in the above exercise) beginning at a low note initially where it does not strain your throat. Then go up the scales, and keep going. As you go up the scales your voice extends lengthening your vocal chords getting thinner the higher you go up. Remember to remove all pressure from your neck. Don't "think high" when executing the higher notes up the scale. "Think high" is a term my opera coach used with me to explain, that if you are not fearful of the note, and don't realize it's "too high" of a note to hit for your register, then you will not strain your neck or vocal chords by anticipating it, but instead, you will expect to just execute what your vocal chords are naturally able to accomplish with proper preparation and exercises practiced. A baby learning a new skill does not think about whether they can accomplish their goal in crawling, walking, running, eating solid foods, they just do it unless they are taught to fear it, and even then they still press through to learn because they are oblivious to failure. Even if they do fail, they get up and try again until success is attained. I'll never forget watching my son learn to walk for the first time, and he was a little unstable at first, but you could not convince him he was not going to make it from one end of the couch to the other! Imagine embodying that kind of drive at its purist and developing it over your lifespan. What is it that you could not do?

There's nothing like the persistence of a no quit kid. It puts me in the mind of my children when they expect something, and persist to get it. Even if they are denied their request, they believe at some point if they hold onto their desire, and persist to achieve their goal in getting what they want, that their expectation will be granted. Do you believe you will get what you want accomplished? If the answer is yes, then you're already moving forward in your desire. If the answer is no, which I don't think it truly is, because you would not be taking the liberty of reading my book. In either case, keep reading! Don't think- just execute!

Motivation

The average singer should be able to sing smoothly through two and a half octaves with no breaks, squawks, or squeals in their voice.

Make a note to yourself during the process of this journey of becoming a stronger singer with these two statements in which you will fill in the blanks:

"I want to improve my voice because:
_____
_____."

"If my voice were as strong as I wanted it to be, I would
_____
_____."

I always instruct my students to listen carefully and repeat what they hear me doing.

Finding Your Voice

Singing competitions and social media videos gone viral have changed the landscape for singers. Great speaking and singing is not about being the best, but about being unique. Being your unique self is being the best because no one else can be you better than you! So enjoy the quest of mastering your unique voice and tone with confidence, control, and power, and share your gift with your audience! Once you find your unique voice, you want to practice vocal exercises that will strengthen your voice, develop specific areas of your voice called registers, and be able to feel the differences of these areas when you sing. As you practice you will utilize and be able to tell the difference between your chest voice, your face voice (behind your nasal area), neck voice (throat), gut voice (diaphragm) and falsetto (head voice). You will also know how to navigate smoothly through several octaves without pressure or strain. Believe me your entire body gets involved in this process. You may get to curling your toes and rolling around on the floor like Patti LaBelle…just kidding, or maybe not…moving on…

Finding Your Tone

You want to be able to improve your singing to produce a beautiful tone. Two basic components of singing are your pitch and tone. Discovering your natural tone will help you define your tone to create a more unique tone that is all your own. Although great singers influence other great singers, I often tell my students to sing using their own voice and not to try and imitate anyone else's sound as their identity. To really find and strengthen your tone you need to be able to sing fluidly in range and in proper pitch. Flexing your singing muscles will help you hear your tone as well as when placing your larynx into proper position. One of the biggest factors in discovering your tone is opening your mouth (nice and big) and dropping your jaw.

Maintaining Tone

It is very important to keep an open and even tone. You must relax in order to open up your tone. Practice keeping your jaw relaxed. Remember not to reach or strain for anything. Practicing the scales and lip and tongue trills help you broaden your octave range when singing and is good for helping you to reach those higher octave ranges.

Lip and tongue trills loosen up everything going up the scale. When recording with singers I often have them do the lip and tongue trills to help them get over the hill with ad-libs and parts of the song where they need to deliver it in a higher octave. This helps with modulations and such. Keep your tone fluid when capturing emotion and in emptying yourself out because it demonstrates control and power, and when you are confident you can deliver, you hear something special.

I have a "Low Quiet Voice Technique" which I also call, "The Soft Technique" that helps to develop your falsetto.

Example:

(Very quietly) Ah ah ah ah ah ah ah ah (4x)

When singing in your lower register, you want to be as relaxed as possible.

Why the Soft Technique?

"How I like to si----ng out"
The Soft Technique mixes your natural voice with your falsetto.

Be open voiced, with an open throat for open tone. Maintain the tone and pitch of your voice by singing softly, while relaxed, then slowly gain more power taking good breaths in the process. Keep your tone steady and pure.

Sing slower, quieter, and softer to be able to hear yourself keeping your tone steady, then you can tell technically what is going on rather than when you sing louder faster and with full power. When stretching your voice, it automatically increases your range. Vocal warm ups on the scale with "Ha ha ha's" help with staccato.

Finding Your Range: Octaves and Categories

When I am working with one of my students and I want to discover their vocal range, I will sit them at the piano with me and after a good warm up (and while in proper posture of course), I will go up and down the scale with them usually beginning at middle C (unless their voice tells me something different), and I will know their range capability at the time based on when their voice fades during the scale.

Categories:

Soprano (1st and 2nd) - Higher female voice

Alto (1st and 2nd) - Lower female voice

Tenor (1st and 2nd) - Higher male voice

Baritone - Lower male voice

Bass - Lowest male voice

Fine-tuning Your Pitch

We all know what it feels like to listen to someone sing off key or out of tune, especially if we are in a small confined space with nowhere else to go.

This is why pitch is absolutely essential for great singing. Pitch refers to the notes and sounds that we hear when someone sings, and it determines if the song is going to sound great or not. As the singer, you will have to maintain pitch in a song with a relative amount of accuracy in order to be in tune with the overall musical accompaniment and harmonies.

Training ourselves to recognize pitches and intervals, to vocalize various notes as well as correct ourselves when we go off key is imperative for achieving an accurate pitch when singing. So when delivering a song, it is very important to study the pitch of the song so you are as accurate as possible. When I encounter a student with pitch problems, I remedy this with pitch correcting exercises.

Pitch

Pitch is a high or low frequency. When you sing, tone is the color of the pitch. Pitch is staying on key with the note. Executing great pitch is listening and matching your voice with the note assigned or being played. I don't believe people are actually pitch or tone deaf, because I have some students that don't know how to arrive there initially and slide up or go completely off key, but learn how to find their way back and nail it on the first try. Tones vary. You can tell a warm tone that is rich depending on what the song calls for. Your tone will convey and interpret the song stylistically. Dark tones can reflect a different story. Your tone on a song can open up the subject and mood of the song. Gospel songs sing the good news of Jesus Christ and are generally delivered with purity and sincerity. When you are communicating hurt it can be a warm but dark tone. Tone is how you color the pitch or note. How do you apply that color and emotion? Pitch is very important in painting the picture of your song so you want to stay in key. Always look at the context of what the song is to determine your approach and then tell the story.

Rhythm

Rhythm is pretty much the beat or groove of a song that you have to keep up with throughout the duration of that song. If you're constantly trying to catch up with the beat of a song, it is an indication that you need to listen more and work on your breathing and delivery technique. To be able to have a fantastic sense of rhythm, again you have to learn some singing basics, such as how to recognize diverse beat durations, to vocalize your notes with various beats, and be able to hold onto the basic tempo of a song.

Mouth Movement: Annunciation and Diction

One very crucial key to singing success is proper mouth movement. Executing great mouth movement such as shaping your vowel sounds and articulating your consonants, along with great posture and breathing will help you achieve sounds and phrases with accuracy, power, and control. Practice singing with a wide open mouth and exaggerate mouth movement in slow motion to get used to singing with precise annunciation and diction. Using your vocal chords as the instrument it is will help you get in tune with pronunciation, annunciation, and diction. Your mouth movement and emotional connection to a song enhances your delivery and the impact you have on your audience.

MASTERPIECE was the group I was in in the 1980's that Norman Whitfield produced, and I was able to exercise my skill and really develop as a songwriter, producer, and vocal producer working with my group.

We had a member named Bobby Jones who was a tenor and I worked with him to just get **power** out of him. And with another member named Michael Foley, he had the voice, but I spent time with him working on **pitch**. I would just push him and drive him, and work on **annunciation and diction** and how to remain **focused**. So I worked with the group for hours a day for about a year before we recorded our record.

I was fresh from leaving the Tempts (Temptations) and had learned so much from all that I experienced there so I knew we had to be ready to deliver before we began the recording process. I wanted to do better with the group and help us get to a certain level that was not only record ready but performance ready. Unfortunately there were a few business decisions that halted the album after its release, but there was great potential there and I will never forget the blessing of that experience.

CHAPTER 2

Voice Strengthening and Singing Correctly

Skill. Strength. Excellence.

And the Child grew and became strong in spirit, filled with wisdom; and the grace of God was upon Him.
+ *Luke 2:40*

Then this Daniel distinguished himself above the governors and satraps, because an excellent spirit *was* in him; and the king gave thought to setting him over the whole realm.
+ *Daniel 6:3*

Therefore send me at once a man skillful to work...

+ *2 Chronicles 2:7a*

1 Moreover David and the captains of the army separated for the service *some* of the sons of Asaph, of Heman, and of Jeduthun, who *should* prophesy with harps, stringed instruments, and cymbals.

6 All these *were* under the direction of their father for the music *in* the house of the Lord, with cymbals, stringed instruments, and harps, for the service of the house of God.
+ *1 Chronicles 25:1, 6*

Q: Let's say there is a singer who comes to you, who has been singing incorrectly and has suffered some vocal cord damage as a result. How would you address the issue?

A: Well for this student, I would ask them to go to their doctor and let them take an evaluation to see if there are any nodes present and stuff like that, and if prayerfully they're not, then I could show them techniques that could correct and help them change and sing properly. I would just need to know what kind of damage that has been done if that is the case.

Also, my breathing technique is so powerful in healing, and I've used it after going through cancer treatments and all that stuff. And then I've had an operation where they used a knife and cut me open, and to assist in my healing process, they gave me a tube to blow and breathe into, and I had to do this for a week or two to build my lungs back up. That experience makes me think about how God breathed life into man and that is impactful to me. Breathing is life!

You are extending life as you breathe and are getting strong. One of the techniques that I use is relative to how a swimmer jumps into a pool, and uses all their muscles to swim. That's how it is with singing, and the techniques I use will require you to use all of your muscles at some point. You will use every ounce of what you have, as far as your diaphragm works, and how all of your physiology works together.

Variation of Scales

Scales are the best exercise for voice strengthening, finding pitch, and finding tone. There are variations of scales you can apply to strengthen your voice, and develop power and control. I will begin by introducing you to a few scales I have developed for working with my variation of voices through my students.

HOW TO DELIVER A SONG WITH IMPACTFUL EMOTION

First, you begin the scale by singing big, before transitioning into soft voice. For developing power and control you want to vary your application of technique preparing your voice to deliver in an amazing supernatural way! Ok let's go...

4x4's Slower tempo with Higher octave =
Higher degree of difficulty.
4 up the scale, 4 back down the scale

Faster and lower with scale variation = lower degree of difficulty.
8 count on each, 8 on end or 4 at start and 8 at end

(For examples of Scales, please visit
www.supernaturalvocals.com
in the tutorial section to see the exercises there)

Big and small delivery of the scale helps you to decrease vibrato and gain more control.

Singing Correctly:

1. Breathing properly
2. Confident
3. Relaxed
4. Taking a comfortable pace
5. Good timing
6. Good posture
7. Keeping a focused mindset to execute delivery
8. Line by line:
    1. emphasizing words
    2. building momentum and
    3. selling emotions
9. Execute mood, pitch, tone, and maintain control on climax of song

Singing Incorrectly:

1. Not breathing properly
2. Thinking "high"
3. Tension/stiffness in the body
4. Rushing
5. Off rhythm
6. Bad posture
7. Distracted
8. No distinction of delivery throughout various parts of song
9. Going:
    1. flat
    2. sharp or
    3. Monotone (no variation of tone)

Singing is like lifting weights. The average person doesn't start off lifting 150 pounds. Usually the bar, the basics, are just enough to develop your vocal chords initially. When equated to vocal training, on how to get power and strength in your voice, you get them through scale repetition, to which you can vary the workout for the outcome you need to achieve. Practice repetition of scales. No matter the genre, scales are the best thing to do to get the right pitch, measure tone, and get control.

I practice the scales in succession that will stretch your voice, strengthen it, and develop more power. I change the process of the scale first doing a soft delivery then building up to a louder delivery, then I go back down to soft, and build louder again just enough to feel it and build your breathing and lung capacity, which helps you get control. Be careful not to strain and go too fast. I usually go slow first then speed up once the muscles are acclimating. It is important that patience is your virtue in the process of development.

CHAPTER 3

Developing A Listening Ear

The Art of Listening

"Listen to advice and accept instruction, that you may gain wisdom in the future."
+ *Proverbs 19:20*

"Like a gold ring or an ornament of gold is a wise reprover to a listening ear."
+ *Proverbs 25:12*

"Know this, my beloved brothers: let every person be quick to hear, slow to speak, slow to anger."
+ *James 1:19*

"Let the wise hear and increase in learning, and the one who understands obtain guidance."
+ *Proverbs 1:5*

Q: How did you learn to develop a listening ear, and how does it impact your delivery?

A: Well first of all I was forced to develop a listening ear by first challenging myself to listen. I would study an artist that impacted lives, especially Donny Hathaway and Stevie Wonder. Well how did I develop a listening ear? In order for to me deliver and do the things I was not able to do at the time, I had to study the artist and really focus and listen.

I would put the speaker up on a table and close my eyes and listen over and over and over again. First you just hear a song, but then you listen for hours and you hear the drum line pattern and why the vocal is doing this here, and strings doing that there, and you understand more about movement and how to breathe like that. You'll learn how to control vibrato and then by continuing to study and listen, you will get insight as to why the bridge is done in the way it is, even to how it transitions in. Listening helped me how to count more like the rhythm of a heartbeat, and as I experienced, it just becomes more and more alive to you during the process of listening. There is really an art form to listening.

DEVELOPING A LISTENING EAR

Q: Is there anyone you can think of that was just a really great listener?

A: No. Most people don't understand what it means to listen. I had to develop that gift myself. If you want to be a perfected artist, you have to understand how to listen. I learned from Nat King Cole diction, Donny Hathaway power, Stevie Wonder, a lot in different areas.

As I listened more I started having breakthroughs!

Training Your Ear to Listen

When I first started working with artists and in helping them to develop, I would put two speakers on a table, and have them listen to artists like Donny Hathaway.

When you hear certain love songs that are happy, for example, one of my favorite love songs by Donny Hathaway is "Take a Love Song and Sing It." I started out listening to the music and the piano and then doing in depth listening to how he breathes when he delivers/sings one line. I hear the breath it took to finish a line. When you study a song long enough, you start to hear the nuances that make the song what it is. For example, like the marriage of a voice to the guitar or piano, helps bring out the vocal, which is in itself an instrument. As you listen to a song and study it, you start hearing that every little instrument has meaning. The more you listen in depth, the more you set the atmosphere for your emotions to come forth. Emotions are developed through relationship, intimacy, and experience. When you are influenced, or impacted by an experience, or song, it will be that much easier to interpret and exude that through your vocal performance. Emotion creates texture and an atmosphere conducive to its fluidity. Then the music begins to tell on itself, like in how the piano player felt when he played just by the way his delivery sounds. You will then become in sync with the orchestration of the piece. Be mindful of this in your song selection. You will hear meticulous pieces of the song delivery which will impact you to convey emotion. You become a part of that experience and it becomes a part of you, and you begin to understand why these lyrics were chosen, and the evolution of the song in how it was written. Immersing yourself into this process will teach you how to develop as a listener and bring another listener into this very experience by the way you color sound on a painting. You will be able to do this instinctively as you grow through practice and practice, being able to pick up on the mood of a song.

Connecting Emotion

Take a listen to the following songs I've written and have also vocally produced that display emotion:

Sailing by Lakeside

I Wonder Where You Are Tonight by Rose Royce

Shine Your Light by Rose Royce

Can You Believe by Robin Thicke
(To see another example which is of an unreleased song "If U Ever" I performed that displays emotion, please visit
www.supernaturalvocals.com
under the Tutorials tab.)

It's so important to get this blueprint of emotion... where you take your time when you hear songs like Otis Redding's "Sitting by the Doc of the Bay" and Aretha Franklin's "You Make Me Feel Like A Natural Woman," or Mahalia Jackson's... well anything on Mahalia Jackson! (If I Can Help Somebody).

You want to become the picture of the character that is painted through a song. When you learn to listen you will begin to have an expectation and gain the ability to capture moments.

Capturing Emotion

Even when in the recording studio when the artist becomes one with the song, you have to capture that moment where it captures the epitome of the song. Sometimes it's the first take. You are looking for a certain experience take after take, and then the artist has to internalize it, and keep it, and manifest it, and then it's not about thinking, but about becoming that emotion in that moment. It's a vulnerable place that is transparent and you have to surrender to allow yourself to get there and remain there. That's why a creative person has to work to stay focused, not allowing distracting thoughts in that will take them out of that place where they can capture that moment when expressing their art. It's a portrayal and story to tell.

HOW TO DELIVER A SONG WITH IMPACTFUL EMOTION

I am listening for lyrics that will impact me emotionally whether I am going to feel happy, romantic, remorseful, or repentant, or bold and encouraged or brave. You may feel and want to express a myriad of emotions simultaneously. You have to be able to empty yourself out and be used as the vessel with the gift God created you for.

Norman Whitfield, *couldn't sing, but he was able to get that* **emotion** *out of people when producing them because he would get into the studio and man... he had so much emotion! It was so powerful to witness him in action. Norman had so much vision and knew what he wanted to hear and feel and experience on a record. He could take any voice and bring emotion out of it. He found a way to capture what a person had inside of them and pull it out and connect them emotionally. He was a master at that. Norman Whitfield had one of the most amazing work ethics I've ever seen.*

Endowment and Escape

When I pray to be used by God, I have to go before Him and empty out with expectation that He will use me. If I pray, I'm gonna pray without ceasing, and pray till I know my prayers are being heard, and pray pouring myself out. The impact of this type of delivery is perpetually impactful.

What does listening do? If you were confined to a wheelchair and couldn't go anywhere, you could put on the music and go soaring.

You're listening to learn...and then impart what you've learned into others. This is one dynamic of the beauty of the art of listening. There are so many places you can go. It's a study within itself. You can put your ear to the speaker and just listen. You can travel to many places through listening. Just think about the art of meditating on the Word of God. What a gift! Hearing is believing.

Stretching Your Hearing Capacity

As you develop your listening skills, you will interpret what you hear with an impactful execution. Mastering the skill of listening requires the practice of listening and studying where you want to be. Listen to breathing patterns, endings of a line, and resolve. How does one sell the song? What is so captivating about the pronunciation, annunciation, and diction of vowels and syllables, and certain words and phrases delivered? Approach the song with a level of emotion and intensity that requires you to have to go to a place where it resonates with you. Pick the right song for your voice and if you are given a song for an audition or for a project, study it.

Technique is important, but don't be too technically perfect to where you miss emotion and the opportunity to be impactful with your delivery. You have to have an edge that goes beyond technicality sometimes. Technique is vital but you have to balance. You can master them both where you don't loose impact on your delivery. With technique, vibrato can be controlled. Sounding commercial means limiting vibrato. Lyrical content and melody and translation of it, the interpretation thereof…you will begin putting those pieces together in a deeper way. The artist conveys a song like an actor conveys a script. Study!

Meditating for Hearing, Timing and Articulating

The Art of Listening is a meditation process. Not transcendental méditation, but meditation that requires a distinct listening practice, which brings you to a peace to better interpret. Articulation is another key to singing correctly. How you mouth and articulate affects your sound style and flavor.

Listening not only brings peace of mind for your learning process in delivering your own interpretation of a song, but it also compliments, and enhances the delivery process of any collaborating vocalists who can play off of your skillful performance.

Listening enables you to attack and deliver at the right time which is relative to rhythmic placement and timing. As you anticipate singing your song, before you begin delivering the first line of your song, which I call your entry, listening will help you learn how to count better, and apply the proper time placement of your line. Is your timing 4/4 or 3/4 timing? Sometimes you may deliver a song that has a timing which is slightly off-kilter, which is great to be able to execute a timing such as this because it truly enhances your artistry and vocal prowess. Practice listening to learn how to anticipate the entry of your song relative to the timing of that particular piece.

Rhythmic placement for a vocalist, is very much comparable to rhythmic placement for a dancer, and rhythmic placement for a musician. Just imagine yourself dancing to the music with your vocals as a dancer moves to the music and finds various counts to deliver moves, which after much practice becomes natural. Imagine your voice as the additional instrument which compliments the music composition you are a part of.

The practice of your vocal exercises may feel like an aerobics class, but the execution of what you practice vocally will feel like the dance performance of your life! You can even incorporate the flare of freestyle as you feel it! Can you see yourself there? Choreography and freestyle both take skill, and there are many styles you can incorporate in one piece, but to be most impactful, you must execute with skill, fluidity, confidence, and passion! The most impactful dancers execute skill with impactful emotion.

Your hearing and delivery become one when you can paint colors on lyrics and put meaning to them through emotions as you feel how it comes to you, spending less time thinking about it while in real time and actually executing the communication happening throughout your vessel. Listen to how you want to communicate to the listener. I like to make reference to film and soundtrack. For example, like what action is in the beginning of a movie that makes the viewer sit down and watch, is what delivery is in the beginning of a song that will make the listener stop and listen.

CHAPTER 4

Song Interpretation & Delivery

Delivering Interpretation

But I discipline my body and bring *it* into subjection, lest, when I have preached to others, I myself should become disqualified.
+ *1 Corinthians 9:27*

By faith we understand that the worlds were framed by the word of God, so that the things which are seen were not made of things which are visible.
+ *Hebrews 11:3*

And Pharaoh said to Joseph, "I have had a dream, and *there is* no one who can interpret it. But I have heard it said of you *that* you can understand a dream, to interpret it."
+ *Genesis 41:15*

Q: Ok, let's just say you are in the airport and you run into a singer that is familiar with your vocal program, and asks while in passing, "Can you give me some advice on what I should do on this audition (or first recording, or live performance) to make an impact?

A: First, that's 3 different questions, but I would say for an audition, know what you are going to do, and study as much as you can and be confident in what you have to present. Then it would depend on what the audition is for. For a reality show or for a music group, or stage show, etc. I would say study and find out what the expectation is and how successful candidates impressed in the past. How does one impact the judges? They key is taking on confidence from live performances to recording in the studio. Take the gift that God has given you and impact the world with it. Because it's not just about you, its about the lives you are affecting with the gift and talent that you have. And when you look at it in that regard, it's like wow!

What does music really do? There's a saying that it soothes the savage beast, and really, music is healing. It was created to heal because when you understand why God created music, which was to worship Him, then you understand as a worshipper so many miracles happen from that experience, so music really is powerful, and it is important just as with any gift that it is used the right way to empower others. When you have a winning mentality, you can't lose regardless of the outcome because all you are thinking about is winning and losing doesn't enter your mind. You never lose, only learn! Learning creates more opportunities. Seek and find them! If you give everything you have when delivering a song, it's IMPACTFUL. Just give it all you have!

Song Interpretation and Delivery

During the course of time I spend coaching my students, I engage them in exercises and dialogue that help them evoke emotions for interpreting a song. I then give them tips on transferring this technique to anything they sing. In addition to expressing emotions, there are key emotions that as a singer, you need to evoke in your audience to make them like and believe you. In the infamous words of Jesus Christ, "Fear not…" Never be afraid of becoming transparent before your audience, bearing your all. A vessel unafraid is a very productive vessel. I also teach my students how to use their anxieties to their advantage through emotion and stance. Remember that there is always a way to win! When you have the victory in the first place, how can you not win?

Instead of singing too calculative and safe, let go of what you have inside of yourself. You will hear me say this in one way or another on a consistent basis because it is key to impacting your audience, including yourself.

When you sing courageously, the freedom you find will also free others who are on the journey with you as listeners and students of your gift. So without apprehension, free yourself and others by bearing it all in total transparency.

Ok now let's continue….

Think about how to make your voice convey your passion, your convictions, your affection, or your intentions. My vocal lessons are designed to develop your vocal chords and teach you how to master control over your voice production muscles and synchronize your basic singing techniques in which you will see the results within minutes, days, weeks, months, and years.

What's mostly important is helping people unlock the key to their emotions and teaching effective exercises that exist for opening up the voice to all its possibilities.

My vocal lesson's teach you techniques that enable you to discover and access parts of your voice you've never been able to reach, and that you might not have known even existed. In the event you encounter performance anxiety, I encourage you to overcome it by confronting your fear and taking charge of the situation. You can make great progress by doing so hence letting go of your anxiety.

Interpreting emotion in a song is like acting, you have to feel it. For example, if I got a letter from my son saying he went off to be in the army and I didn't know it, I'm not going to be melancholy or straight faced in my emotions. I am going to (in a distraught, sad and dramatic voice) be like "Oh no my son left and didn't even tell me- he just wanted the freedom!"

Also, you've seen these commercials selling soap. Well you don't normally wash in the shower with such jovial expression, but that makes you want to buy the soap from the excitement interpreted by the actor selling the soap with their body language. Their expressions are animated and convincing that they are having fun in the shower with this soap. Emotions emitted in how to sell and convey are used more than you realize. Politicians, salesman, and performers use emotion to convey their thoughts all the time.

Don't start a song at the climax, unless the scene calls for it like a chasing scene in the beginning of a movie. Build and let the listener take a journey with you.

*Working with **LEVI of the Four Tops**, I remember was a little weird starting off because I used to think he was a vampire, because he only came out at night and slept during the day. But once Levi got in the studio, I found myself being in awe because he listened and his **interpretation**, God rest his soul, was so amazing. He really got it. I worked with everyone, but when Levi got behind that mic, it was something to see.*

***WILLIE HUTCH** was a consummate professional and I didn't think he needed anyone to produce him, but watching him and Norman (Whitfield) communicate, left me spellbound. To see someone pronounce words and **interpret** a song I wrote in the way he did just blew my mind. He sang it like he wrote the song, and he added to my song and didn't even want credit.*

It's an amazing feeling to see someone take a song that you wrote, and just deliver it in such a dynamic way. It was exciting to see how he just grabbed **emotion**. He took a song I wrote called, Paradise, and he did something with it I didn't even do. My experience with Willie Hitch taught me something about a deeper level of selflessness, humility, and just being giving. He was a great songwriter who was so **humble** and giving. I was truly humbled by his presence.

Song Delivery

When you first hear a song you like, what is the thing that draws you in the most? Could it be the melodies? The lyrical content? The vocal tone and delivery of the artist? The music? Well, most of the time a song that draws you in consists of all the above likable traits. To first be able to deliver a song in its purest form, is to first be able to interpret and understand every word of every line to the song. You sing a song in steps because there is a process to delivering the song in the most impactful way. Each section of the song builds first generally with the intro, then into the verse, or sometimes the chorus depending on the structure and arrangement of the song. You gain even more momentum with your chorus after the verse with a vocal climax, and then you take your listener even further in their experience with the bridge and colorful ad-libs you add. Usually the musical composition has turnarounds after every 8 count, in which you can mirror that count vocally.

The entire song content from musical arrangement to the melodic structure to the lyrical content is called a body of work. When singing a particular song, no matter what the genre, we must take the time to understand the nature of the song. What is the meaning of the songs storyline and what effect will it have on the world and the artist who is delivering the song? There are songs of empowerment that are powerful enough to start a movement of change in a culture. Songs of inspiration, that stir up your very soul, even impacting a spiritual event in your life, or many lives, motivating us to achieve more than what anyone could fathom. There are songs that inspire or encourages a person or nation to overcome adversity. There are songs that move people to change their beliefs or empowers their faith.

The process of conveying a body of work to successfully impact the world through the artist delivering the song can be pretty amazing to experience. Stay the course and complete the work. Every line is pertinent in this process.

For example:

When performing a gymnastics routine, if you stumble through the routine, how you dismount can really make a great impact. You know you have a great delivery when you come out of a chorus/hook part of the song and then go back to the verse and it is just as powerful (impactful) as the chorus. That's when you know you have something special, when you get back to that second verse and the momentum has only grown. The ad-libs on a song are what I call the icing on the cake...the sprinkles!

Blueprint of Emotion:
1. <u>Take</u> your <u>time</u>.
2. <u>Give</u> <u>all</u> you have in your delivery.

<u>Two Examples of Pieces Displaying Great Emotion:</u>

Song: ***A Change is Gone Come*** by Sam Cook
Speech: ***I Have A Dream*** by Martin Luther King Jr.

Capturing the Moment When Recording

When I worked with the legendary Norman Whitfield, he used the expression, "Squeeze the Charmin's!" In other words, pour it all out and give it all you have emotionally. You have to express internalized emotions. Emotion to delivery is an art. Portraying the character, interpreting the language, fulfilling the assignment, with all sincerity, with uninhibitedness, for delivering an impactful emotion.

HOW TO DELIVER A SONG WITH IMPACTFUL EMOTION

CHARLIE WILSON once recorded a song in his apartment. The record label tried to get him to record and duplicate the song. But they couldn't capture all of that **emotion** that he **delivered** on that original recording in his kitchen. I mean they put him in the big studio and all that but it just wasn't the same, so you know what they did? They ended up using that same recording from the kitchen of an apartment because of the emotion that was **captured** there.

When working with **CECE PENISTON,** it was incredible because she is an artist that has so much **power and confidence**. She was really a sweet person, and I was introduced to working with her by my good friend Emanuel Officer, who also worked with her along with Robbie Neville and Bradley Spalter. I'll never forget working with her because she was an artist who could just **deliver**. I enjoyed producing her vocals because at the time, we had a chemistry of emotional expression. She was a dynamo when delivering **emotion**. Back then we had things that could EQ the voice and we could add certain effects, but it was nothing like what is out there now. It's like many people use auto tune and just rely on auto tune, which is not good when you want to convey real emotion.

Singing as an Anointed Vessel for Jesus

How do I master what I do? By immersing myself in it. If I run, I run and run and run and run and run. If I write, I write and write and write and write and write. Once you give all you have it's impactful. Don't try to sing too perfect or safe. Take the chance of taking the full journey and allow your listeners to take it with you. What are you listening for? Is it to escape, to gain your freedom?

The Song Dynamic: Structure

To understand a song and deliver it, you must first break down the structure of the song itself. Most songs usually start off with the verse first, which sets up the storyline. The verse explains what is going on or introduces the subject matter in the beginning of the song. Most times, when singing verses to a song, you kind of start off low key or subtle enough to entice the listeners ear to draw them in. The melody, or melodies to a song are so very important to set the feel. The next section of the song is usually the pre-chorus, or pre-hook. Every section has usually 8 bars unless it's a rap record. The pre-hook is always the part that sets up the hook (chorus).

What I mean by this is that the pre-hook section takes on momentum coming out of the verse setting up the hook or chorus, building energy wise and takes the melody up a higher notch, so by the time you reach the chorus/hook, the song explodes in a climax.

The next section of the song which we call the chorus or hook, tells you what the song is all about. The title of the song may or may not be included in the hook, but the hook is usually sung with the most power and energy. However, some songs chorus's or hooks can be subtle yet still impactful depending on the story. Now after the chorus of a song, the song returns back to the verse, usually starting over with the same or a similar melody as the beginning verse, yet may be a little more elevated melodically, so as you progress to the second time you sing the hook, your delivery is even more impactful.

Usually, after the second hook comes the bridge, which is kind of a release that reinforces the song itself as far as the storyline and melody goes. The bridge for most singers, allows more vocal expression, which also demands more power, even in song and lyrical content. The bridge explains more in detail the why, when, and how of the song. This is the basic structure of a song no matter if it is in the genre of RnB, pop, Gospel, rap, classical, etc. However, when it comes to creating, you can create a masterpiece that breaks all the rules!

CHAPTER 5

Confidence, Control, and Power and How to Nail An Audition, Live Recording, and Performance: Ending on a High Note

Confidence. Control. Power.

Being confident of this very thing, that He who has begun a good work in you will complete it until the day of Jesus Christ;
+ *Philippians 1:6*

For we are His workmanship, created in Christ Jesus for good works, which God prepared beforehand that we should walk in them.
+ *Ephesians 2:10*

Now to Him who is able to do exceedingly abundantly above all that we ask or think, according to the power that works in us,
+ *Ephesians 3:20*

I can do all things through Christ who strengthens me.
+ *Philippians 4:13*

For God has not given us a spirit of fear, but of power and of love and of a sound mind.
+ *2 Timothy 1:7*

Blessed *are* the meek,
For they shall inherit the earth.
+ *Matthew 5:5*

Death and life *are* in the power of the tongue,
And those who love it will eat its fruit.
+ *Proverbs 18:21*

He who *is* slow to anger *is* better than the mighty,
And he who rules his spirit than he who takes a city.
+ *Proverbs 16:32*

Developing Power and Control by Working the Scales

Do the scales moderately. Do soft voice then big...ready? Remember, always breath taking good breaths, be relaxed and have good posture.

Ah ah ah ah ah ah ah ah (Soft Voice)
Ah ah ah ah ah ah ah ah (Big Voice)
Ah ah ah ah ah ah ah ah (Soft Voice)
Ah ah ah ah ah ah ah ah (Big Voice)

Now do the reverse of that...ready? Do big voice then soft. Get your breathing, power and control. Let's go!

Ah ah ah ah ah ah ah ah (Big Voice)
Ah ah ah ah ah ah ah ah (Soft Voice)
Ah ah ah ah ah ah ah ah (Big Voice)
Ah ah ah ah ah ah ah ah (Soft Voice)

GOD GAVE ME THIS TECHNIQUE!
No other coach is doing this!

Record yourself so you can monitor your tone. You want to be relaxed but will need to change your posture to convey different delivery. In this exercise you will get very tired using your lung capacity. Do no more than 30 minutes of that, even still gauging your movement so you do not overextend your vocal chords. Do the reverse process afterwards so you don't get bored and sleepy. You will find yourself getting stronger and stronger over time. When practicing this scale, you will keep yarning and I also bet you will sleep well for the night.

The higher you go up the octave of the scale, the more difficult it will get. Do a repetition of 4 normal scales first, then go into these scales soft-big, and then big-soft. This workout is for vocal strengthening and developing power. The big and then soft patterned scale is more difficult than the soft to big patterned scale. When you go slower you will most likely get 2 in instead of 4 in, unless you are a supernatural being of course...like, just kidding, not really. Seriously, this is a very difficult task to accomplish and this is really where your developed lung capacity will come through for you. It's a great workout as well. For example, if you are a runner, you want to take in consideration whether you are sprinting or running the long race by laps. Prepare your vocals for the execution with the proper training. Going slow at first allows you to measure and equate where you are vocally, revealing your strengths and weaknesses. After you do these soft-big and big-soft scales, go back to the regular scales I first introduced you to earlier in this book.

Here is another scale pattern to help you increase in power:
Ah ah ah ah ah-1-2-3-4-5-6-7-8- ah ah ah ah
(Hold for 8 counts)

In addition, when you go up for the 8 count, crescendo with a little more power at the climax before you come back down at the last 4 count, then draw back in for control to practice your breathing and vocal delivery regarding control and power. By doing this, you are giving your vocals a good stretch.

Go up the scale then down the scale, once each time.

(4x4's) Slower Tempo:

Ah-1-2-3-4-ah-ah-ah-ah-1-2-3-4-ah-ah-ah-ah-1-2-3-4-ah-ah-ah-ah-1-2-3-4-ah-ah-ah-ah

(4x4's) Mid Tempo:
Ah-1-2-3-4-ah-ah-ah-ah-1-2-3-4-ah-ah-ah-ah-1-2-3-4-ah-ah-ah-ah-1-2-3-4-ah-ah-ah-ah

(4x4's) Fast Tempo:

Ah-1-2-3-4-ah-ah-ah-ah-1-2-3-4-ah-ah-ah-ah-1-2-3-4-ah-ah-ah-ah-1-2-3-4-ah-ah-ah-ah

If you want your voice to sound fresh and radio friendly, then execute the control this scale will give you which will also help you get rid of vibrato.

Don't get this exercise confused with the sliding technique. Using the sliding technique with scales has to be practiced so you know how to do it, so you don't belt it out and harm your vocal chords. Remember, even a voice that is weak and frail can still deliver emotion. Work your muscles.

If you execute this scale properly, you should be tired and sleep well at night. Walking on the treadmill, jumping rope, and exercising on a regular basis can be great for improving vocals. However, you have to do the right program for you! Consult your physician if necessary on the best workout for you. Cardio and stretching are good exercises to get the blood flowing and oxygen flowing throughout the body. After all, singing is a workout for the vocals and the rest of your body!

A Winning Mindset

A pivotal aid in an impactful delivery is mindset. Before you step into a room, you have to have a winning mentality; especially if it is a song that will uplift people. You have to have an uplifting mindset regardless of how you feel at the time. You must momentum build when delivering a song.
Godly Confidence

A common problem I've seen with singers in the studio, is exhibiting **LITTLE FAITH,** *where they question themselves and hinder themselves from embodying the confidence to do certain* *things that I knew they could do, but they didn't even realize was in them to do. I've seen this over and over and over and over again. So I am like, hey listen, you've just gotta reach in and quit thinking so hard and let go! You can't try to manufacture emotion and feeling. I've seen where the artist would start off good and then by the end of the line lose the delivery and the emotion. It was like they began to fall off a cliff and I'm like, uh uh, no, let's finish it, let's finish it strong. See, when you get good, and get happy and excited, you can lose focus, like when Peter was walking on water and began to sink when he started thinking. (Smile). The important thing to remember is to take that first step of faith, which will lead to your next step, and then the next step, and as you are strengthened with each step, you experience another breakthrough!*

When working with great professionals in the studio, you have to be careful sometimes because some of the greatest talents are so sensitive, and you have to use discernment when communicating to be most effective, and to capture that emotional delivery. Even when working with greater singers than myself, I still know how to get them to deliver.

The foundation of my confidence is in the Lord. When I think about all God has brought me through, all I can say is, "Thank you Lord!" My confidence is truly in Christ Jesus. Before... I was arrogant because of my insecurities, and now I am bold in Christ because I understand my value in Him, and the purpose of my gift of His power operating through me.

Practice makes perfect but you have to practice the right way. Singing is a methodical process and you have to practice to build your confidence. The Word of God says you have to study to show yourself approved! The Word of God also says in the multitude of counselors there is safety. So when I want to be great, I surround myself with great people. You can't go into something with a defeated attitude or false humility. If you do, you will learn that pride eventually leads to a fall. You must be authentic, and you must go in with a winning attitude and mindset. The Word of God says that God has not given us a spirit of fear, but of power, love, and a sound mind. You've gotta be bold and on it gifted person! Get your help, and with what you know, get understanding from listening and application.

To achieve greatness, you should be the consummate student. The more you know, the better you get. Study a song for hours, and once you learn it, then make it your own applying your own style through your delivery. Having confidence is knowing your strengths and weaknesses, and knowing Who makes your weaknesses His strengths, and then working to have a clear understanding of your goals and having a blueprint and foundation and format of what you want to accomplish, why you want to accomplish it, how you are going to accomplish it, when and where you are gonna accomplish that goal. A winning mentality is believing in yourself. If you start off with a defeated mentality then you're going to lose because you have already opened up the door for loss to come in. I don't do that! Philippians 1:6 let's me know that I can be confident God will finish His work in me and through me. I am confident that His Word abiding in me, will accomplish what He set out (purposed) for it to do. I have an expectation! Faith is a gift as well so hone your measure of faith to acquire more of it. You can do this through continuous study.

When you know a thing, you are confident on how to do it. If you want to be a great singer, you have to have a voice. If you can talk you have a voice. If you can hum, you have a voice. If you can whisper, you have a voice. Where is my range? How low? How high? What are my strengths and weaknesses? Ask yourself these questions and work on the result of what you discover through study and application. The miracle of singing is directly connected to the ability to feel from your soul. I have seen some amazing wonders of ability defying the odds because of faith and hard work. When you discover your weaknesses, study someone who is strong where you are weak. I instill confidence in my students and artists I work with which allows them to do better and accomplish more.

How did I develop a good relationship with tone, and in maintaining my tone for taking it up the scales? Well, I am a spinto (raspy) tenor. I demand attention with my voice when I sing because I sing with edge and confidence. I believe in myself, and the gift God gave me because of my relationship with Him. I am humbled by God's grace who is the giver of the gift I am confident in, because I am confident in God and I trust God. I am human with frailties but I know my God is able to do anything and I am His vessel. I am inspired to do great things and find those great things in the people God puts in my path.

When I first met the artist **TREASURE DAVIS,** *her* **tone** *was fascinating, and she had a meekness about her character. I noticed that when we began working together, she had some* **power**, *and I wanted to bring out more of that power. I always thought to myself, if she should put that tone with confidence and power, without thinking while in the studio or performing, but instead just releasing that power, letting go, and reaching deep down to get that emotion, then all that would translate on a record and she is really going to have something special. I would always challenge Treasure to develop vocally. She could sing, and I could sing, so I would challenge her to do runs, and build her* **confidence**. *I would do a run, and then challenge her to do the run, and all of a sudden I noticed she became so competitive like I was. She developed even more so as a vocalist and songwriter while growing in confidence, and she was ready to be in attack mode and go! That's one thing I can say about her, is that she went from that mild mannered quiet person to this monster! She became a conqueror, and by having Jesus Christ, was able to go out and deliver.*

The Blessing of An Honest Self-Assessment

*As I first began writing songs for record placement, my mentor **NORMAN WHITFIELD** would challenge me after hearing me sing my songs. After the very first time I sang one of my songs for him, he asked me, "Where's the hook?" I said, "The hook?" Then he said, "Yes, you know the part of the song that repeats itself, the chorus?" That conversation was the conversion of my status as a songwriter with potential, to a songwriter with placements on the Billboard charts. I just needed to apply a key ingredient to my formula which unlocked the journey of a successful songwriting career.*
Whit taught me how to be truthful with myself, and to never settle for mediocrity. He taught me how to say what I had to say with complete honesty, and to never be afraid to be different in my approach to songwriting.

Spending time around veteran songwriters like **BILLIE CALVIN**, and **MILES GREGORY**, and other writers who were **greater than myself**, allowed me to witness the great **emotion,** patience, and understanding they executed when creating their songs.

I remember spending time with **WAH WAH** (infamous guitarist) and I would be songwriting and he would hear something and be like, "Uh uh, no, that's not it." I would be like, "Huh, what do you mean?" But I learned how to become better by taking in **constructive criticism** and learning from it.

Always take an honest assessment of where you are, and where you need to be. The only person to stop me is myself, so I am going to move out of my own way by doing what I can to sharpen my technique and mechanics, as a perfectionist, and become great, and that's basically the way I feel about it. I challenge you to share my perspective for yourself. Apply what you know at each level and then progress to the next step. Confidence is in steps. Study on how to get better in strengthening your voice. I say to myself, "I am more than a conqueror!" I execute the Word in confidence and my gift in confidence... which is a process.

The **process** for me goes like this:

1. Receiving the gift
2. Understanding Who the Gift Giver is, and growing in my confidence in Him
3. Having confidence in the gift from the Gift Giver
4. Stewarding over the gift that He has given me the ability to express through my vessel which He created in His own image. God makes no mistakes!

Planting the seed through laboring the field, watering it by giving it love and nourishment, and trusting that God gives the increase is a powerful combination. You must trust and let go to tap into the supernaturalness of your gift! I've written songs on the spot from being confident in the gift God has given me.

Be Your Unique Self

Don't imitate to duplicate someone else's gift. I have a gift of helping others find their unique gift in their voice and in themselves.

I was in the Temptations for a short season and when I auditioned for the spot, they said,
"Hey aren't you a little young?"
But then I said, *"Yes, but do I still get a chance?"*
And they said, *"Sure go ahead, and sing*
Donny Hathaway's A Song for You."

I studied Donny Hathaway, so I tore that song up and was able to make it my own... and I made the group. I mean I was able to go up in my falsetto and capture the emotion. After I finished singing that song they asked me to sing something else. They asked me again, *"What else do you know?"* Because I went in there with confidence and didn't do just the bare minimum, my audition was impactful because I committed to giving it my all! I closed my eyes almost the whole time. The only thing they told me was to open my eyes more. So I learned to capture emotion and focus with my eyes open to master the performance.

It's not about all the power and runs you have but it's about timing and placement and using what you have. When you have confidence, you are ahead of the outcome and can navigate easier. Fear not! When you have an understanding, like in a relationship, the essence, the timbre of your voice... connecting your confidence to your delivery...will help you arrive to something great! Close your eyes and meditate, and then make sure you open your eyes once you master that place so you connect with your audience on an audition or live performance. You have to go in like a special task force because what you get out is what you put in. If I shoot 500 free throws a day and someone shoots 200 free throws a day, whose average will be better? Now if I shoot one thousand free throws, my percentage is going to be that much better.

TAMYRA GRAY *is a friend and artist I've worked with who has an amazing voice! She has a strong identity as an artist and after we finished battling it all out, she let me hear a song we did called, Your Love is Like Water, and it blew me away! She reminds me of a baby Whitney (Houston) but she is definitely her own person. She has a beautiful voice and range and sticks to her artistry instincts. She is an artist, songwriter, and actress who is confident in her performance which opens doors for her gift. I truly believe that there are no limits to what Tamyra can achieve as she uses her God-given gifts to glorify Him.*

SOLANGE *is an established artist who I've also had the pleasure of working with. I admire her as an artist and songwriter because she always had her own niche, developing her artistry to the next* *level, while successfully coming out of a great shadow from her infamous sister. She represents her own unique self and is winning with that. She created her own mystique and went with a 60's type of vibe. Solange evolved into her own identity and into the artist we see now. I respect her for that.*

Don't fear or be intimidated by another person's gift. There's always somebody more skillful than the next person. Like in a western, there's always someone faster, but it's about using what you have. Another side note (from the Bible) is that the race is not given to the swift or the strong, but to those who endure to the end...to the finish. Let that be an encouragement to you as you work hard to become more skillful. I had to wait for hours before I got my audition opportunity, but I knew I had what it took for the job. I was nervous but at the same time I had an expectation. I wondered about things such as, "What is the expectation of the person auditioning me? Do I qualify?"

Most importantly, I studied the material and I knew <u>my</u> voice. I knew how to sing their songs and deliver with confidence. I understood that all my practice was about to pay off! I was in attack mode by taking all that nervous energy and channeling it to accomplish the emotion I needed it to because I was honest with myself. That's a good way to redirect nervousness, anxiety, and overcome fear, by understanding your assignment and going in once again like a special task force agent to complete the mission.

The Mock Audition:
Building Confidence in a Room Full of Decision Makers

*Embody these **tips**:*
1. Make **good eye contact** and exude confidence. Remember, you have a **winning mentality**.
2. **Take your time**, while tuning your ears (**listen/discern**) for precise rhythmic timing.

3. Be sure of your delivery and **stick to your instincts**, don't change the game plan especially if it is not called for, unless you are determined to **outperform yourself**.
4. Let your posture convey to everyone in the room that **you've got this**! **Confidence** coupled with **humility** and **skill** is attractive. An impactful **delivery of emotion** is intriguing leaving your audience wondering where you are pulling it from. It makes people root for you!

Embrace your moment! Debunk doubt with reckless abandon! Don't think too hard, it's all about doing now.

Helpful Technical Tips:

1. <u>Open up</u> your mouth and <u>round off</u> your words and phrases.
2. Utilize your <u>vessel</u> for <u>placement</u> of <u>texture</u> and <u>flare</u>: Sing from your <u>diaphragm</u>, pushing through your <u>chest</u> (when necessary) then up through the <u>throat</u> (when necessary or for grit but do carefully so you don't tear your vocal chords or develop nodes) and <u>head</u> (for falsetto).
3. Concerning your <u>lower tone</u>, which is more airy... give it a little <u>rasp</u> at the top of the note, and <u>round out</u> the syllable to add <u>edge</u>- don't think about it.

Yes, in one line you can sing from the diaphragm to the chest to the throat and to the head! Finding the mechanics that are best for your voice, for where your voice is, and displaying your vocal strengths, is a journey. Think about it initially, and once you master it, don't think anymore, just do!

Ask yourself, "What is my purpose for showing up?" As a follower of Christ, the attitude I exude is: "Thank you for allowing me to affect your life with the gospel of Jesus Christ." That is what I am thinking. Why? Because the Word of God dwells within me, therefore I take Christ wherever I go. The love that I exude from my vessel derives from my love for God and my love for people.

Also ask yourself, "What about my presence is contagious?" A smile, authentic expression of emotion, kindness, transparency of heartbreak, grief, and confidence are all contagious!

When you use all those dynamics at once, it takes a lot out of you! That's why singers sweat and work it out! Preachers of the gospel do the same. You are gonna need stamina for the long haul!

Ready...set...

What about your <u>stance</u>?
Are you <u>ready</u>?
Do you have one foot <u>forward</u>?
Are you in <u>attack</u> mode?

Let's go!

Wisely Take A Chance

Now, in continuing with attitude... If you are enthusiastic, and you are giving it all you have, then it will be received that way. Becoming transparent is what an artist is! Don't be so calculating. Jump out of the box and flow. There's a way to be technical without it getting in the way of creativity and delivery. Find the balance as you practice and master what you learn. Keep learning. Go off the grid and take some chances, but at show time, know what you are doing... don't go too far off the grid if you are not sure about your landing. Work your strengths.

What can you do to shock yourself and step out of the box? What do you do when you wanna reach someone and make them feel what you feel? Confidence plays a big part in answering these questions. Engage the process, befriend the process, and confidently execute your understanding of this process.

Delivering impactful emotion is relative to the Word of God when Jeremiah said, "It's like fire shut up in my bones." Impactful delivery of emotions are not manufactured, rather, you have to pull them from somewhere. If you try to do this (manufacture emotion), at some point it will run out and tell on itself. Think about something that will take you to that emotional place.

I think about God's amazing grace over my life when singing the song *Amazing Grace*. Do you know the story of the song? Can you interpret what the song means to you? Sometimes it's hard to fathom the heart and emotion of someone else, so you have to find your own.

(In reference to the songwriter of Amazing grace), *"Will God forgive me for all the wrong I've done?"* Yes God will. True repentance allows a sinner to receive the gift of forgiveness. The expression of gratitude for this grace is penetrating and can be overwhelming. This is why Gospel music is so impactful to the singer and the listener.

Emotionally Overwhelming Circumstances: Amazing Grace

Amazing grace, how sweet the sound, that saved a wretch like me! The sound of grace is so sweet when it's saving you! I was lost and blind...thinking about it (God's grace) brings me to tears because I think about all the wicked things I've done in my life and how God forgave me so now I am free! Freedom from burden and guilt and shame and bondage.

I can worship freely, casting my cares upon Him (Jesus) because he cares for me. I could not pay the price it cost to redeem me. I am thankful for the atonement through Jesus Christ, and my singing should exude that without having to think about it because it's a place where I actually am, and I am bringing listeners along for the journey. No matter how your voice is: soft and delicate, or strong and powerful, emotion can be expressed. Taking what you have and becoming transparent with vulnerability is key.

HOW TO DELIVER A SONG WITH IMPACTFUL EMOTION

Gospel Interpretation

In the song "Give Me A Clean Heart," I am thinking about God's Holy Spirit surging through me with power healing people through my vessel. Once you get a touch, like touching the hem of the garment of righteousness of Jesus-...let me get the residue of Peter's shadow who has the faith from walking with Jesus. Let me increase in faith.

Solomon was wise because he asked God for wisdom instead of wealth, but he already obtained some form of wisdom by learning about God from His father David, who was after God's own heart. Are you keeping company that can inspire you to become your very best? How are you going to ask for something you don't know about? God is able to fashion the heart of His children to desire the things that are good. You have to learn and grasp it and ask for what you know you can have because of your confidence in not only that it belongs to you, but that you will receive it when you ask, seek, and knock.

Live Recording and Performance

When recording your vocals, you have to learn how to capture the moment where emotion pours out in a magical way. When performing live, you don't have time to anticipate, because there are no do-overs. You have to get it done on the first take.
Also, take advantage of the enhancement provided by the microphone. The microphone is a good way to get power! Mic placement is key!

If you start off big... you'll end up small. If you start off small, then you will finish big! Now if you breathe you will have power. If you don't breath, you won't have power. Mastering breathing techniques will help you sing strong and funnel the breath to where you need it to go to get the sound you need.

How do you accomplish recording and auditioning? By being free. By having faith that your hard work will produce fruit. By believing you can deliver! By trusting and being fully surrendered.

Levels of Difficulty and Putting It All Together

When I was in high school, I was in football and track, and during the off season, for a short season, I did gymnastics. I learned about the advantage of delivering based on the degree of difficulty.

You can do an iron cross...but what if you did an iron cross and then an iron L, then did an Olympic cross and handstand back-to-back? That's crazy! My point is, it's not always about doing what someone else does, but about how you put your particular routine together. Even being in a place where you were stumbling through a routine, having an amazing dismount could actually change the outcome of your results and the impact you have on the judges, which will then increase your favor!

It's a journey, it's never a fast race. You must get enough wisdom and knowledge on how to run a marathon. Sprinters don't run marathons when it's time to run sprints, and marathon runners don't run sprints in a marathon. You are not gonna sprint all the way through a song when singing. Keep building and stacking upon what you learn. If you go about it the right way, what you learn will not only stand, but it will compound and live off of the interest. That is food for thought.

The Business of Recording

How do you get back into things mentally when you have the pressure of a deadline? Applying repetition of what you've learned in the clutch may surprise you. Being coached through it can be invaluable. Expect to capture something amazing within the moment of spontaneity.

That moment a person was there (emotionally) at a supernatural level, and captured it, well, it may not happen like that consecutively, which is why you want to practice delivering at a superb level so moments like that are more frequent. In some cases, it was the moment. You may never feel like that again.

Stepping Out in Faith

The reason I love gospel music so much, is because I love Who the Gospel sings about! I know that the benefit of walking by faith and not by sight with God in Christ Jesus is that He never changes, and that is solid ground to stand on! I can trust that. I trust that His Holy Spirit abiding in me will take me where I need to go! And when I am there, I am not just ministered to emotionally, but also physically. Worship and walking in purpose is healing!

This example of faith is the difference between those who make a bigger impact and those who don't because they play it safe. You have to step out in faith which is sometimes the hardest thing to do. In order to get a return on your investment, you have to first invest! How else can you enjoy the benefits of compounding interest? You may not know how you are going to get there initially, but identifying you have a place to get to will help you get there. Pick the vehicle that is best suited for what you are trying to do. If you stay on the safe side when it comes to delivering, then you are going to be safe, and that is the extent of it. You have to step out.

When a creation understands its purpose, and functions in its purpose, it communicates that purpose bringing about clarity and peace to the beneficiaries for which it was created for. Expressing its purpose it was created for ministers to the creation as well by enabling it to operate in its function. A car that is not driven will decay. Faith that is not exercised will decrease. Be diligent and keep the faith!

CHAPTER 6

The Attitude of An Impactful Singer With Winning Work Ethics

Humility + Diligence = Distinguished

Continue earnestly in prayer, being vigilant in it with thanksgiving;
+ *Colossians 4:2*

Then this Daniel distinguished himself above the governors and satraps, because an excellent spirit *was* in him; and the king gave thought to setting him over the whole realm.
+ *Daniel 6:3*

Blessed *is* the man who endures temptation; for when he has been approved, he will receive the crown of life which the Lord has promised to those who love Him.
+ *James 1:12*

Whatever your hand finds to do, do *it* with your might; for *there is* no work or device or knowledge or wisdom in the grave where you are going.
+ *Ecclesiastes 9:10*

And do not be conformed to this world, but be transformed by the renewing of your mind, that you may prove what *is* that good and acceptable and perfect will of God.
+ *Romans 12:2*

Q: Why do you believe so many artists/singers who are confident, also express arrogance? How can one avoid this?

A: Wow. Well...arrogance is over confidence. Imagine this...you know you have a gift and you hear your music over and over again through mainstream media. Then you notice that others want to be like you, dress like you, wear their hair like you, walk like you, sing like you, talk like you... and then you realize you have this impact on other people's lives and instead of being humbled and appreciative and responsible about the impact of your gift, you become like, "Oh wow look at me?" "Look at how good I am and look at what I'm doing?" And then you lose focus of your true purpose and identity succumbing to the attention from the actions of others you observe.

People have tendencies to put you on a pedestal and give you accolades and make you like an idol. In fact, they indeed make you an idol. And then it becomes like a worship to you. In fact, they practice idolatry by worshipping you. They seek to worship you, and it becomes worship to man by man. You have to be careful about that. There is no humility in that.

There's that false humility, but there is not that true humility. You have to really be careful about listening to others who build you up because the influence of power can streamline those compliments right into worship. People look at you and then you in turn look to yourself, which is a very dangerous thing.

When using your gift, you may experience the temptation that is ever-present to look to yourself, and away from God, while out there performing in front of people, earning enough money to buy houses and cars and relationships, leading you to be deceived in your perception, that you are independent of God, or even that you are more powerful than God, when in actuality, God is the only One who is all sovereign and has the power to give life and take life and usher our very souls into eternal life. Having all the money and power in the world cannot give you life or extend your life should God decide to take your breath away or translate you home.

Songwriters are not always in the public eye, but they can get carried away with pride because of the power of their songs in which they are writing and placing.

The Bible says that pride goes before the fall. And then from a spiritual aspect, the enemy (Satan), the devil, said in Isaiah and Ezekiel, "I will ascend on high and be like God." Iniquity was found in Satan and look at what he did, he was a cherub and then iniquity was found in him. Oftentimes the spirit of vanity creeps into man. There was an artist named Vanity, whose life was transformed by the Gospel of Jesus Christ, and she evangelized the Gospel with her powerful testimony until God called her home! It is good to humbly serve the Lord with gladness.

*I've spent over 20 years with **ROBIN THICKE**, and just watching him, as an artist, I can clearly see how he's touched so many people through his music, because he has really reached inside of himself and **delivers emotionally**. I think I've learned just as much from him as he has learned from me. Us just hanging out and co-existing together, it came to a point with his delivery where I told him, "Hey man, you gotta just not care." Robin was able to travail through things he experienced in life with music and just get the emotion out. Working with Robin was interesting as he was on a quest, and he still is, and he developed to be quite a **good listener** because he didn't stop with what I taught him, but he worked even harder to study and find the right tone to use as well as the word/lyric and the delivery. Robin is also very **disciplined** when it comes to his artistry. I've watched him get up in the morning with a cup of coffee and his paper and pencil going over lyrical ideas and thinking outside of the box. He would just sit at the table, going over concepts and applying words that ignite a spark of another idea, even until the wee hours of the morning. All night long... getting into the zone. I expect that in this new season of his life and career, he will evolve into even a greater artist, with a greater impact, because he is true to his artistry, and his hunger to learn, revolutionize his connection between his artistry and his audience, while reinventing himself is very much of a driving* factor. Imagine what Christ could do with an amazing gift like Robin's?

ELLIOT WOLFF (God rest his soul) who was one of my best friends, was the epitome of a **genius**. He was literally a scientist, sampling trash can tops for records, and was as **meticulous** as could be. I've never seen anyone with his **work ethic**. He's worked with Aretha Franklin, and Chaka Khan and so many more artists. He also produced me and took me to another level emotionally, which I didn't think was possible at the time. He was such a perfectionist and I love and miss him dearly. You don't find people with a mind like his every day.

JAMIE JONES is an extremely gifted, humble, and anointed friend of mine who I've worked with for many years. It's pretty interesting to work with Jamie because not only is he a gifted songwriter, producer, musician and composer, but he is also a legendary artist who is still actively using his gifts as a lead singer in the Pop/R&B group All-4-One and has also released a gospel album. What amazes me the most about Jamie is his love for Jesus Christ and his humility, which I know is the reason why he continues to impact the lives he does, and enjoys the success he does today.

SAM WATTERS, also one of my dearest friends, is all around lyrically, musically, and business wise spectacular, and I've learned from watching him, (while also witnessing the chemistry) working alongside the brilliant **LOUIS BIANCANELLO,** pull that something out of everyone no matter the artist or genre. Sam is a mastermind of marrying sounds, matching genres and interpretation, and is one of the most incredible vocal producers that has ever lived...and by the way we are super competitive at everything with each other! When it comes to songwriting, arrangements, textures, sound, and how to find a niche for an artist, Sam is one of the best! He is well rounded, ingenious, and has a gift in pulling that special something out of an artist. He knows how to get the best outcome from a situation. He has a smart business mind as well. We worked with so many artists together helping them achieve their goals of success. Being a former artist himself (Color Me Badd) he knows how to perform and what to look for.

I am blessed to be around some amazing minds including my friends **WAYNE WILKINS, THOMAS DAWSON, JACK KUGELL, ERIC JACKSON, GREG PAGANI** and so many more, whose work ethics rival their God-given gifts.

ROBERT "ELIJAH STORM" DANIELS

CHAPTER 7

The Anointed Vessel: Connecting Your Gift to its Purpose

Anointed for His Purpose

"Everyone who is called by My name, Whom I have created for My glory;
I have formed him, yes, I have made him."
+ Isaiah 43:7

This people I have formed for Myself; They shall declare My praise.
+ *Isaiah 43:21*

"You are worthy, O Lord,
To receive glory and honor and power;
For You created all things,
And by Your will they exist and were created."
+ *Revelation 4:11*

But rise and stand on your feet; for I have appeared to you for this purpose, to make you a minister and a witness both of the things which you have seen and of the things which I will yet reveal to you.
+ *Acts 26:16*

Make a joyful shout to the Lord, all you lands! Serve the Lord with gladness; Come before His presence with singing. Know that the Lord, He *is* God; *It is* He *who* has made us, and not we ourselves; *We are* His people and the sheep of His pasture. Enter into His gates with thanksgiving, *And* into His courts with praise. Be thankful to Him, *and* bless His name. For the Lord *is* good; His mercy *is* everlasting, And His truth *endures* to all generations.

Psalm 100

The God factor (The Holy Spirit)

When singing the gospel, you should be factoring in the Holy Spirit in Christ Jesus so you can turn everything over to God. Don't get that confused with emotion and delivery. What I am talking about now is the anointing of God, and you, His vessel. Emotion is a part of the make-up that makes us who we are.

As an analogy...if you are being used by God, as a cup, when you are already filled before God pours into you, then you are consumed with yourself, but when you are a cup emptied out and decreasing yourself...allowing God to use you, by letting go and giving it over to God, then you flow in the power of His anointing. Humility enables you to be used by God. It is an honor and privilege to be used by God. That's important to know and understand when singing gospel; that Jesus died for your sins and by our Heavenly Father's grace you are saved through faith in Him who the gift was packaged in.

When you are worshiping in gratitude, something amazing happens. You have become the word that you are singing and the Word of God says "My word will not go out void." You change lives with your gift, and by stewarding that gift to develop in skill, as David did as a shepherd, and as a musician and psalmist. With the proper attitude and application, you can move mountains with God! You can be used as a great vessel with a great Foundation, so have an expectation and turn it over to Him so lives can transformed forever. Fasting and praying is a great way to prepare when ministering in song when you want to make the greatest impact because it keeps us in a sensitive place to God's voice and His Holy Spirit.

Praising the Lord

Discernment is listening, and seeing. Listening to the voice of the Lord, seeing what He reveals to you, and wisdom is displayed as worship by obeying His instruction. Humility of knowing we need the Lord's guidance is required to represent Him in His power. Honoring God on your knees in prayer, and becoming so humbled by His presence through our worship...is honoring God our Father. Christ in the Garden of Gethsemane had solace in prayer and was listening for His Father's voice.

God uses nature to shout His glory, but His Holy Spirit may also speak to you in a still small voice. God may choose to speak through any vessel of His choice. There are no limits in God.

Romans 11:36
For of Him and through Him and to Him
are **all things, to whom** *be* **glory forever. Amen.**

Psalm 150
Praise the Lord!
Praise God in His sanctuary;
Praise Him in His mighty firmament!
2 Praise Him for His mighty acts;
Praise Him according to His excellent greatness!
3 Praise Him with the sound of the trumpet;
Praise Him with the lute and harp!
4 Praise Him with the timbrel and dance;
Praise Him with stringed instruments and flutes!
5 Praise Him with loud cymbals;
Praise Him with clashing cymbals!

**6 Let everything that has breath praise the Lord.
Praise the Lord!**

When I sing for the Lord, I have spent time in prayer and then I empty myself out. Sometimes I even pray while I am ministering in song. God anticipates the prayers of my heart because He has fashioned them Himself.

A foundation of faith helps you master the art of interpretation, supernaturally. How? By being in communion with the Supernatural God. Those who worship Him must worship Him in spirit and in truth. You can't see the wind but it's there. You can't see the mechanism that operates but you can feel it when you encounter it. Ok, so let's get back to pouring yourself out. The effectual fervent prayers of the righteous availeth much; so imagine taking the steps to seek God diligently when operating in your gift. Seeking God brings great rewards from Him. Take ahold of it! Keep at it and the fruit of your labor will take root and spring forth!

Pressing through various dimensions is a supernatural occurrence ignited by faith. Did you know the angels assigned to us gain power from our worship? Hallelujah!

Q: What is your advice to a person who wants to get into the music industry for the first time, or who has been through a traumatic experience, but wants to hang in there? How would you advise them to avoid pitfalls and succeed in the music business?

**Psalm 51:10
Create in me a clean heart, O God,
And renew a steadfast spirit within me.**

**Hebrews 4:12
For the word of God *is* living and powerful,
and sharper than any two-edged sword,**

**piercing even to the division of soul and spirit,
and of joints and marrow, and is a discerner
of the thoughts and intents of the heart.**

**Titus 2:14
who gave Himself for us, that He might redeem
us from every lawless deed and purify
for Himself *His* own special people,
zealous for good works.**

A: I would strongly encourage them to have a God-fearing support group around them, close enough to them where they are being held accountable for their decisions. They should also establish and maintain fellowship with the body of Christ through a church location which is considered a home base. Even if they are traveling most of the year, there should be some relationship built that can be called upon frequently as the word of God instructs us not to forsake the gathering of the brethren, so we are not sifted like wheat by the enemy, and so we are not deceived by our own thinking.

The devil will attack your mind, and thoughts, and persecute you so that you will be weak in your faith in God, and in Jesus Christ. Because the reality is, the devil wants you to serve him! If you come from a good church background and you learn about your gifts, where they come from, and how to use them, then that is a good start. Then, by receiving support from mature Christians in the faith, you will not fall into the snare of self-glorification, but you will glorify God with your gifts.

The Bible instructs us to train up a child in the way that they should go, so when they get old, they shall not depart from it. Put together a good management team that has a good background in work ethic, integrity, and of course humility, and who are grounded in the Word of God. You have to have balance and keep focus of bringing glory to God and not just to yourself. It's so easy for man to find something other than God to worship. Staying the course will help you greatly because we all fall short, but God also says when we fall, He will pick us up.

It's better to fall in Christ then to rise with the devil, because God says the humble shall be exalted and the prideful will fall. So you don't want to be in bondage but you want to be free in Christ and help others to be free in Jesus as well.

Q: When did you come to realize that you are an anointed vessel in the ministry of music and in sharing your testimony for God's glory? How are you connecting that to your talent and purpose?

A: I didn't realize it for a long time. Well, I did begin to understand that I was set apart by God because of the attacks from the enemy I suffered as a young child. When I was young I had a lot of dreams. I can recall all the spiritual attacks and things that were happening in my life back then, you know? As I grew older, I realized that there was a calling on my life. I realized that when I sang, it was a gift, because like songwriting, it came easy to me, and I noticed the impact that my gift had on people's lives.

I remember when I was 17 I got into trouble and went to jail, and instead of putting me with the juvenile's, I was put with the adults. In my cell, I began to talk about Jesus Christ. I was scared at first, but then when the Word started to come forth out of me, everyone in the jail began to sit there like they were children. And I don't remember what I spoke, but I know Jesus was with me then like He is with me now. Even after all those years, I know that nothing can separate me from His love. Then I remember one of the guys sleeping in the top bunk who was big and muscle bound, got up and gave me his bed while he slept on the floor.
When I first got in there, everyone was looking at me so I felt intimidated. But God was with me in there and He was there before I got there.

I always studied the Word even as I got older and was in the church. But I stayed in the Word and had God's favor and grace in spite of my own bad decisions. You know like Joseph, and not like I am comparing myself to him, but yeah, my gift made room for me wherever I went because God enabled it to do so. I knew I was hedged by God.

My thirst and love for the Word developed my gift of discernment of spirits which shows me people and their intentions towards me, and God continues to show Himself faithful as I abide in Him. Even when I ran from Him, His grace and mercy covered me! He's given me that gift of discernment. He would reveal to me the wolves in sheep's clothing who wanted to prey on my enthusiasm and curiosity and He protected me. He will do that for you!

Romans 8:28
And we know that all things work together
for good to those who love God,
to those who are the called
according to *His* purpose.

Q: How would you advise a person who wants to get into the music industry? Would you advise them to get into the music industry? And if so, how would you help them connect to their purpose through their music? What would that process look like?

1 Thessalonians 4:7
For God did not call us to uncleanness, but in holiness.

1 Corinthians 14:12
Even so you, since you are zealous for spiritual *gifts*,
***let it be* for the edification of the**
church *that* you seek to excel.

Deuteronomy 8:18
"And you shall remember the Lord your God, for *it is* He who

gives you power to get wealth, that He may establish His covenant which He swore to your fathers, as *it is* **this day.**

A: I've always been surrounded by young people because I look at the purpose I have as a songwriter, even reflecting on the times when I was being mentored by Norman Whitfield, and the influence and impact he had on me. Whit (Norman Whitfield) left the door wide open for me to succeed in the music industry. My intent would be to give them caution first. The music industry, as with the entertainment industry, is not for the faint of heart because it will eat you up. There is wickedness abounding all over the place in that industry, so you have to be careful about everything you do to the company you keep, the things you say or repeat, and be aware of the influences that surround you physically, and spiritually even more so.

I am more aware than ever before of the influences on my life...so when I run into people that endeavor to make music their career, I kind of guard them and take them under my wing and show them, this is the way that you approach the industry. I am able to by God's grace on my life, by my walk, let them see who I am and help them find balance, and there is the decision that has to be made on whether or not you are going to compromise your faith, your morals, your family, and relationships for what the music business is offering you.

I've been offered wealth and opportunity for greater fame, to which I made the decisions to turn them down on a number of occasions. Why? Because the Bible says, "What does it profit a man to gain the world and lose his soul?" What do you have to pay, and what do you have to give?

You have already been bought with a price, purchased with the blood of Jesus Christ that He shed for us. He became a ransom for us, so we would not be judged for a debt we could not pay for or ever afford, but it's His grace that saves us through our faith.

When the sorcerer came to the disciples he offered to pay for the anointing because he wanted to use it for magic and for his self-glorification. Many people get into the industry for the wrong reasons which include self-gain or glorification. While the potential of financial compensation is a major motivator, the promise of fame, power, and influence coupled with a lavish and whimsical lifestyle are superficial and deceiving. Not many speak to the lust of the flesh and the snare that awaits those who are deceived by the lies of the enemy.

Q: Can you be in the music industry, whether in the secular or gospel industry among the top successful artists and executives without compromising to a certain extent?

John 17:14-19

14 I have given them Your word; and the world has hated them because they are not of the world, just as I am not of the world. 15 I do not pray that You should take them out of the world, but that You should keep them from the evil one. 16 They are not of the world, just as I am not of the world. 17 Sanctify them by Your truth. Your word is truth. 18 As You sent Me into the world, I also have sent them into the world. 19 And for their sakes I sanctify Myself, that they also may be sanctified by the truth.

Daniel 1:8-21

8 But Daniel purposed in his heart that he would not defile himself with the portion of the king's delicacies, nor with the wine which he drank; therefore he requested of the chief of the eunuchs that he might not defile himself. 9 Now God had brought Daniel into the favor and goodwill of the chief of the eunuchs. 10 And the chief of the eunuchs said to Daniel, "I fear my lord the king, who has appointed your food and drink. For why should he see your faces looking worse than the young men

who are your age? Then you would endanger my head before the king."11 So Daniel said to the steward whom the chief of the eunuchs had set over Daniel, Hananiah, Mishael, and Azariah, 12 "Please test your servants for ten days, and let them give us vegetables to eat and water to drink. 13 Then let our appearance be examined before you, and the appearance of the young men who eat the portion of the king's delicacies; and as you see fit, so deal with your servants."

14 So he consented with them in this matter, and tested them ten days.15 And at the end of ten days their features appeared better and fatter in flesh than all the young men who ate the portion of the king's delicacies. 16 Thus the steward took away their portion of delicacies and the wine that they were to drink, and gave them vegetables. 17 As for these four young men, God gave them knowledge and skill in all literature and wisdom; and Daniel had understanding in all visions and dreams.

18 Now at the end of the days, when the king had said that they should be brought in, the chief of the eunuchs brought them in before Nebuchadnezzar. 19 Then the king interviewed them, and among them all none was found like Daniel, Hananiah, Mishael, and Azariah; therefore they served before the king. 20 And in all matters of wisdom and understanding about which the king examined them, he found them ten times better than all the magicians and astrologers who were in all his realm. 21 Thus Daniel continued until the first year of King Cyrus.

A: No. I mean you can go in there thinking that, but that's going to change as soon as you elevate and get to a certain level of it, and then you will see what kind of world you are in, and the spirituality of it all is revealed. If you are compromised in your faith, it becomes difficult to run away from the snares, and then at some point, you are going to have to make a decision on who you are going to serve. It happens, it's unavoidable. There's no way around it, unless you <u>don't compromise</u>!

Even when Christ Jesus came into the world...He knew His destiny. He knew why He came, but there were certain things He had to do that His father had established before He came into His earthly ministry. He had to go and fast and pray and be baptized. And in His baptism was a show of submission to God, which we are to follow in repentance to God as we receive the ultimate baptism of the Holy Spirit upon our belief in Christ Jesus. John was the forerunner.

God told John the Baptist to tell the people about someone coming and to repent now! Jesus told John to baptize Him, and then God revealed that Jesus was His Son, in which He was well pleased. When Jesus went into the wilderness during His time of fasting and praying, He was encountered by the enemy Satan, who tried to give Jesus a shortcut to His obedience by tempting Him with Satan's kingdom.

What did the devil show Jesus? The same thing we are being shown as an artist today, which is the kingdom of this world. Temptation is going to present itself through the devil, because when you have an anointing from God, it is sacred and purposed to give Glory to God. But the enemy wants you to take a shortcut away from God and give the glory to him (Satan).

The enemy wanted to stop Jesus from fulfilling His purpose in the Father, which was accomplishing salvation for all by giving His life on the cross, being buried and then rising from the grave on the 3rd day. This was God's plan before the beginning of time. Jesus was resurrected in all power, but if He had given into the temptation of the devil, we would have suffered a great loss. Because of the sin of man, there had to be a sacrifice by non-other than God Himself in the person of Jesus the Christ.

He became a once and for all sacrifice for us all so that we can be a living sacrifice, holy and acceptable unto God. Before Christ, priests would go into the temple with a bell tied around them and when you didn't hear the bell, you knew they fell dead in the presence of God because of their unrighteousness, but Jesus is the sacrifice for us all so we can enter into the presence of God.

His Spirit is available to abide in us because of Christ's work on the cross. So now, can you better understand the devil's objective of getting us to worship him, even if it is under the guise of worshipping ourselves, or worshipping other idols, or anything man made apart from God? Because it is then, where the devil can move forward in His goal of bringing glory to himself. For we know that the wages of sin is death; eternal death; but Jesus came to give us life, and life more abundantly.

The enemy wanted to ascend above the throne of God. God gave him, the enemy, this world but Jesus didn't take that shortcut. He became the sacrificial lamb and atonement for our sins. The world may be growing in darkness, but Jesus is the light of the world through the growing body of believers. Be encouraged!

Q: So what counsel can you give to those who are trying to serve God and serve the demands of the world?

Matthew 6:24

No man can serve two masters: for either he will hate the one, and love the other; or else he will hold to the one, and despise the other. Ye cannot serve God and mammon.

Mark 8:36-38

36 For what shall it profit a man, if he shall gain the whole world, and lose his own soul? 37 Or what shall a man give in exchange for his soul? 38 Whosoever therefore shall be ashamed of me and of my words in this adulterous and sinful generation; of him also shall the Son of man be ashamed, when he cometh in the glory of his Father with the holy angels.

A: Some people just don't care about eternity, or believe in it for that matter. They've made an agreement with the enemy to serve him, or either they have been deceived, giving into the lust of the eye where there will be fruit, but will that fruit be of light or darkness? They only think about the immediate and physical gratification rather than living life for eternity. Eternal separation from God the Father just doesn't matter to them.

Q: What advice would you give to someone wanting to attain success? What does true success look like?

Ephesians 2:10

For we are His workmanship, created in Christ Jesus for good works, which God prepared beforehand that we should walk in them.

Proverbs 18:16

A man's gift makes room for him, And brings him before great men.

1 Corinthians 7:17-24

17 But as God has distributed to each one, as the Lord has called each one, so let him walk. And so I ordain in all the churches. 18 Was anyone called while circumcised? Let him not become uncircumcised. Was anyone called while uncircumcised? Let him not be circumcised. 19 Circumcision is nothing and uncircumcision is nothing, but keeping the commandments of God *is what matters.* 20 Let each one remain in the same calling in which he was called. 21 Were you called *while* a slave? Do not be concerned about it; but if you can be made free, rather use *it.* 22 For he who is called in the Lord *while* a slave is the Lord's freedman. Likewise he who is called *while* free is Christ's slave. 23 You were bought at a price; do not become slaves of men.

24 Brethren, let each one remain with God in that *state* **in which he was called.**

A: The picture of success man paints is self-glorification, and of people following and worshipping them to satisfy their desire to be in control. But true success, Jesus defines as taking the narrow path, and warns us that wide is the path to destruction. You must attain a certain level of discipline and sacrifice and have the love of God in your heart to stand in the evil days.

Daniel 3

The Image of Gold

3 Nebuchadnezzar the king made an image of gold, whose height was sixty cubits and its width six cubits. He set it up in the plain of Dura, in the province of Babylon. 2 And King Nebuchadnezzar sent word to gather together the satraps, the administrators, the governors, the counselors, the treasurers, the judges, the magistrates, and all the officials of the provinces, to come to the dedication of the image which King Nebuchadnezzar had set up. 3 So the satraps, the administrators, the governors, the counselors, the treasurers, the judges, the magistrates, and all the officials of the provinces gathered together for the dedication of the image that King Nebuchadnezzar had set up; and they stood before the image that Nebuchadnezzar had set up. 4 Then a herald cried aloud: "To you it is commanded, O peoples, nations, and languages, 5 that at the time you hear the sound of the horn, flute, harp, lyre, and psaltery, in symphony with all kinds of music, you shall fall down and worship the gold image that King Nebuchadnezzar has set up; 6 and whoever does not fall down and worship shall be cast immediately into the midst of a burning fiery furnace." 7 So at that time, when all the people heard the sound of the horn, flute, harp, and lyre, in symphony with all kinds of music, all the people, nations, and languages fell down and worshiped the gold image which King Nebuchadnezzar had set up.

Daniel's Friends Disobey the King

8 Therefore at that time certain Chaldeans came forward and accused the Jews. 9 They spoke and said to King Nebuchadnezzar, "O king, live forever! 10 You, O king, have made a decree that everyone who hears the sound of the horn, flute, harp, lyre, and psaltery, in symphony with all kinds of music, shall fall down and worship the gold image; 11 and whoever does not fall down and worship shall be cast into the midst of a burning fiery furnace. 12 There are certain Jews whom you have set over the affairs of the province of Babylon: Shadrach, Meshach, and Abed-Nego; these men, O king, have not paid due regard to you. They do not serve your gods or worship the gold image which you have set up." 13 Then Nebuchadnezzar, in rage and fury, gave the command to bring Shadrach, Meshach, and Abed-Nego. So they brought these men before the king. 14 Nebuchadnezzar spoke, saying to them, "Is it true, Shadrach, Meshach, and Abed-Nego, that you do not serve my gods or worship the gold image which I have set up? 15 Now if you are ready at the time you hear the sound of the horn, flute, harp, lyre, and psaltery, in symphony with all kinds of music, and you fall down and worship the image which I have made, good! But if you do not worship, you shall be cast immediately into the midst of a burning fiery furnace. And who is the god who will deliver you from my hands?" 16 Shadrach, Meshach, and Abed-Nego answered and said to the king, "O Nebuchadnezzar, we have no need to answer you in this matter. 17 If that is the case, our God whom we serve is able to deliver us from the burning fiery furnace, and He will deliver us from your hand, O king. 18 But if not, let it be known to you, O king, that we do not serve your gods, nor will we worship the gold image which you have set up."

Saved in Fiery Trial

19 Then Nebuchadnezzar was full of fury, and the expression on his face changed toward Shadrach, Meshach, and Abed-Nego. He

spoke and commanded that they heat the furnace seven times more than it was usually heated. 20 And he commanded certain mighty men of valor who were in his army to bind Shadrach, Meshach, and Abed-Nego, and cast them into the burning fiery furnace. 21 Then these men were bound in their coats, their trousers, their turbans, and their other garments, and were cast into the midst of the burning fiery furnace. 22 Therefore, because the king's command was urgent, and the furnace exceedingly hot, the flame of the fire killed those men who took up Shadrach, Meshach, and Abed-Nego. 23 And these three men, Shadrach, Meshach, and Abed-Nego, fell down bound into the midst of the burning fiery furnace. 24 Then King Nebuchadnezzar was astonished; and he rose in haste and spoke, saying to his counselors, "Did we not cast three men bound into the midst of the fire?" They answered and said to the king, "True, O king." 25 "Look!" he answered, "I see four men loose, walking in the midst of the fire; and they are not hurt, and the form of the fourth is like the Son of God."

Nebuchadnezzar Praises God

26 Then Nebuchadnezzar went near the mouth of the burning fiery furnace and spoke, saying, "Shadrach, Meshach, and Abed-Nego, servants of the Most High God, come out, and come here." Then Shadrach, Meshach, and Abed-Nego came from the midst of the fire. 27 And the satraps, administrators, governors, and the king's counselors gathered together, and they saw these men on whose bodies the fire had no power; the hair of their head was not singed nor were their garments affected, and the smell of fire was not on them. 28 Nebuchadnezzar spoke, saying, "Blessed be the God of Shadrach, Meshach, and Abed-Nego, who sent His Angel and delivered His servants who trusted in Him, and they have frustrated the king's word, and yielded their bodies, that they should not serve nor worship any god except their own God! 29 Therefore I make a decree that any people, nation, or language which speaks anything amiss against the God of Shadrach, Meshach, and Abed-Nego shall be cut in

pieces, and their houses shall be made an ash heap; because there is no other God who can deliver like this." 30 Then the king promoted Shadrach, Meshach, and Abed-Nego in the province of Babylon.

You must sacrifice. Not like idol worship or witchcraft, but sacrificing in decision making to stand for righteousness and not succumb to evil works. You will have to sacrifice certain platforms, portals, and promotions. There is a price to pay for the Kingdom of God, and there is a price to pay for the kingdom of Satan, but Jesus already paid the cost for our salvation so we can enter into the kingdom of God. The enemy offers you the kingdom of the world which is temporary, and of flesh. Suffering persecution, loneliness, and slander is nothing God can't deliver through, because there is nothing too hard for God. But as you walk with God, you will discover that there is great joy to suffer with Christ, because His Spirit which dwells within us communes with Himself, and the Lord is the source of all of our strength. The gratification of imparting into lives for God's glory is priceless. Being clothed in righteousness is a rich life. What are riches? The riches of life are found in our salvation through Jesus Christ. The reward of changing someone's life, and impacting their life to go through the door of eternity is something that you cannot calculate. That is the true gift and riches and it is a gift no one could ever pay for. Your reward comes from God which produces unspeakable joy and peace. Peace and joy are riches. Giving someone hope is a treasure. The enemy gives false hope that runs out when your money runs out or your circumstances are unfavorable. Those are different languages. Perpetuate the gift of hope and speaking life into a person. Peter was able to heal people with his shadow. When we look at the benefits of walking with God, and serving Him alone, there are too many benefits to discover in our lifespan on this earth. The enemy will counter the Word of God with a false or partial truth, a false gospel and present something like, "Friends with benefits" instead of the gospel of truth which teaches us the benefits of obeying God's Word. A counterfeit is not real or authentic.

Q: What is your purpose for what you are doing, as you look back over your career in the music industry to now?

I directed the **PILGRIM CONGREGATIONAL CHOIR** *back when I was in my early twenties, about a hundred years ago, living in Los Angeles, CA. It was a great experience and prelude to my calling in teaching vocal classes in present time. I taught parts and directed the choir in the songs we ministered.*

Philippians 3:7-15

7 But what things were gain to me, these I have counted loss for Christ. 8 Yet indeed I also count all things loss for the excellence of the knowledge of Christ Jesus my Lord, for whom I have suffered the loss of all things, and count them as rubbish, that I may gain Christ 9 and be found in Him, not having my own righteousness, which is from the law, but that which is through faith in Christ, the righteousness which is from God by faith; 10 that I may know Him and the power of His resurrection, and the fellowship of His sufferings, being conformed to His death, 11 if, by any means, I may attain to the resurrection from the dead.

Pressing Toward the Goal

12 Not that I have already attained, or am already perfected; but I press on, that I may lay hold of that for which Christ Jesus has also laid hold of me. 13 Brethren, I do not count myself to have apprehended; but one thing I do, forgetting those things which are behind and reaching forward to those things which are ahead, 14 I press toward the goal for the prize of the upward call of God in Christ Jesus. 15 Therefore let us, as many as are mature, have this mind; and if in anything you think otherwise, God will reveal even this to you. 16 Nevertheless, to the degree that we have already attained, let us walk by the same rule, let us be of the same mind.

A: I want to be able to sow into a life and let them see that there is another way...a better way! There's another option. My hope is to enable them to see the true gifts that they have. When you know better, you are expected to do better; to open your eyes to see the truth. The devil comes to kill, steal, and destroy, but Jesus is the way, the truth, and the life, and came to give us life abundantly. I use my gifts, talents, and passion for God's glory in accomplishing His will for my life. I labor to help others understand the benefits of using their gifts for what God has purposed them for. There is a great reward in submitting to God and resisting the devil. I desire to be an example of God's amazing grace in this world. That's why I am so thankful to not only teach, preach, and create music, but even more so to challenge myself to live my life as a worship unto the Lord, the Great I AM.

ROBERT "ELIJAH STORM" DANIELS

HOW TO DELIVER A SONG WITH IMPACTFUL EMOTION

An Inside Look At My Studio History With...

The Temptations
Norman Whitfield
Rose Royce
The Four Tops
Lakeside
Dr. Dre
Robin Thicke

THE TEMPTATIONS

How did you end up working with the Temptations?

It was through my relationship with Gregory Matter, who was a mutual friend of mine and of the Tempts. Gregory was also one of the singers in the group called Side Effect who had a single out at the time produced by Wayne Henderson of the Jazz Crusaders called, *Always There.* Greg is very charismatic with a winning mentality and always looks for the positivity in a situation. Greg remembered me from when I auditioned for his former group called The Formations. One of the guys in the group who was like my nemesis at the time didn't want me in the group, no matter how incredible I was it didn't matter, he was like, "naw," I guess because it was too close to home as we attended the same high school at Manuel Arts. However, I still maintained my relationship with Greg Matter.

After that experience I went into shedding, which is like when a bear goes into hibernation season until winter is over. I was just practicing vocals for like 8-10 hours a day singing and studying Donny Hathaway, Stevie Wonder, everybody…and just kept singing and studying. One day I got a phone call from Gregory Matter and he was like, "Hey, Dennis Edwards left the Temptations (he was the one who replaced David Ruffin) so can I tell Otis about you?" Otis was the main guy in the group that handled all the outside affairs for the Temptations. So I got a call the very next day from Otis Williams, and he said, "Hey, you know Gregory Matter gave me your number and we wanted to know if you could come to an audition tomorrow?" And I said, "Sure of course." So I came the next day and I had gotten my best friend to take me to the audition.

This is unforgettable because I'll never forget it. I already knew from being around the Tempts with Norman Whitfield what they expected. First of all, you had to be 6 feet tall. I remember when I got there, the room was full. I had to wait over an hour and a half for my audition. The room was so full I had to find a place to sit in the corner. There were people flying in from all over the country and I remember this one particular guy came in and just burst through the main door and knocked on the door really hard and came in with a suit and a briefcase and he said, "I'm ready to take the job!" And I was like, "Oh...this guy came in looking really smart and had so much confidence I mean suited- He actually because of his attitude got picked to audition before the rest of us because it was like basically "Take a number and wait for your turn." But this guy went in after two people, and I still had to wait for like 8 or 9 people to go before my audition came up. But he went into the room and everybody jumped up because he came in there with such a shocking presence, and I'll never forget as long as I live because it was the funniest thing- he went into the room and sang a song by Friends of Distinction called "Grazing in the Grasses of Gas." So he went into the room singing, "Grazing in the grasses of gas can you dig it?" And we were all laughing because with all that hype he was an ok singer. Immediately they sent him out and gave him the door.

So after that- what would happen is you would go into the room, and they would ask you a few questions, and then you would sing. And the song that was the staple song for that audition was called, "A Song For You." Once I finally got into the room, Melvin Franklin, the bass singer, who was incredible, the first thing he asked me was, (in his bass voice) "Uh, how old are you?" And I said, "I'm 23." And he said, "Isn't that a little young?" And I said, "Yeah, but uh, do I still get a chance?" And he said, "Yeah. So we want you to sing, *A Song For You*, do you know it?" They had just had a hit song by my mentor Norman Whitfield, (who taught me how to write), but I knew it by Donny Hathaway, and the piano player for the Tempts knew the Donny Hathaway version so I said, "I know it by Donny Hathaway." He said, "Oh I know that version." So he (the piano player) said, "Ok, so go ahead. Whenever you wanna start you can sing." So he went ahead and played the long intro, the Donny Hathaway intro, and I closed my eyes, (I didn't realize I closed my eyes during the entire performance), and I acted like I was at home in my room with my eyes closed right there in the middle of the room and started singing. I remember I sang the whole song, because they would stop you after about a minute and a half, but I guess they let me go.

So I sang the song, and they were like, "Wow. Can you harmonize?" And Melvin was like, "That was great! We want you to sing something else, you pick it. Do you know any of our songs? But by the way, can you keep your eyes open?" And so I said, "Yeah, ok." So he was like, "What else do you know?" And I was like, "I know every song you guys ever did." So they said, "Ok, let's go." They had me harmonizing and singing in every part. So I just started singing all the Dennis (Edwards) songs, I sang some David Ruffin songs, and then I switched to the falsetto part. I sang "Poppa Was A Rolling Stone, Psychadellic Shack, Cloud 9, you know it was still an audition, so I sang about 3 more songs. You only sang one song during this audition. I believe I was the only one where they actually said, "So what else do you know?" So then I said, "Hey, can I sing some falsetto by Eddie Kendricks?" And they were like, "Yeah, go ahead." So I started singing, "The Girls Alright With Me." So after that, they told me, "Ok you can go back and sit in the living room." They didn't say anything else to me at the time and then I heard them say, "Next!"

There were two other people there with me after the entire audition. The Tempts came into the room where we were and told us all to stand up, and they were like, "You. You come back tomorrow." And there it began.

Immediately, Melvin took me in and taught me about the legacy of the Temptations. He said, "I'm going to teach you about mystique, and about what a privilege it is to be a part of this legacy." And he said, "Oh and by the way, we have a Magic Mountain show coming up, and that's in 2 months, so you have to be ready. So everyday, this is what we're doing- we're rehearsing-...." I noticed something about the Tempts that made them phenomenal. Richard Streets had replaced Paul Williams, the baritone, who was incredible, and who sang that song *For Once In My Life*. Paul's rendition of the song was so powerful; even on stage when they performed it on the Ed Sullivan Show-, everyone was glued to the TV, and I remember he started crying at the end of the song. That is something I will never forget. I noticed that Richard, who took Paul's place, had an amazing voice and very nice falsetto. I noticed that Otis was the one who maintained the character/persona of the group. Otis was like the stabilizer (which we call the anchor) of the harmonies because he could sing every part. Otis could also sing lead. Melvin Franklin, the bass singer, was phenomenal. He had that bass voice and he just demanded your respect. The way he even spoke- he knew when he opened his mouth he was going to get everyone's attention. He definitely got mine.

I remember the rehearsals- how professional they were and how they had the mics and how it was like you were actually doing a show. Even in the rehearsals- immediately from the spinning choreography-, to how they'd put the butterfly mic in the middle of the floor (for the quartet, you know?), I remember some of the most amazing things about the Tempts. They were just incredible and their blending of harmonies-, I've never seen anything like it. Being in groups all my life, I had never even heard of such blends. And if one person would leave the formation to go to the mic to sing a lead, because it was multiple leads, (that's what Norman Whitfield did, multiple leads), the transition was so smooth. It was like clockwork.

So Melvin was like, "When we put on a show, we put on a show. Even when you sweat, (we're always looking at each other when we're performing) when we do like this (wiping his hand across his forehead as if wiping off sweat), to take the sweat off the brow, you do it. Whatever we do as an ad-lib, you do it." It was like a freedom of expression into the choreography. It was one of the most incredible things I had ever encountered because with other groups, you just did the choreography and that's it. But with the Tempts, you had to be cognizant of what everyone was doing, and be aware of your surroundings all the time to remain in synch. And then when it came to texture and delivering a song, to how you carried yourself-, it was remarkable to witness.

I remember there was a man everyone called "Pops", and he was like the choreographer for Motown, and he would come and go over the steps with the group and go over things with us like once a week. He had to be at least in his 70's at the time. But he did this with the Jackson 5, with the Tempts, and with the Four Tops, and everybody knew who he was. He would come and look at us, and tell me how to move my feet, how to be smooth, and how to do this, and how to do that. I learned so much about being professional and about what opens the door to greatness. And I learned about mystique-, to which I had never really heard that word used with artistry before until Melvin Franklin said, "When you walk into a room, you demand everybody's attention. As a Temptation, your stature is tall and how you carry yourself is very important because it's how you look when you walk into a room and how you sit down with confidence you should know, 'Hey I'm a Temptation'." And I always remembered that. That was something that became a part of my personality. Then I noticed the difference of whenever I was around the Four Tops or Gladys (Knight), or around anybody, they noticed me.

I knew how to make people notice me by the way I shook a hand. There's stuff I learned in the Tempts that my father (my stepdad) didn't even teach me. Like how to shake a hand and look someone in the eye. You know Melvin taught me that. Melvin was really instrumental in my development during that time and he was such a great man. The Tempts were everything that I dreamed of them to be and more. They knew they were great people. They taught me to be more confident when it was my time to sing. When it was my time to step up to the mic and sing, it was like, "Take over!" Go in there like gangbusters!

I remember one day, they must've told Dennis Edwards about me (because they were all still friends), so Dennis came up to meet me and heard me sing and said, "If you ever need anything, let me know young buck, I'll give it to you." Even though Dennis left the group there was no drama. I also met Damon Harris who had taken Eddie Kendricks' place, and Damon was from the group Impact (he had started his own group in Baltimore). Dennis would be like, "Young buck, do this." Being in the Tempts was kind of like being in a fraternity. Once you're in the Tempts, you're in the Tempts. It's a lifelong legacy.

So how did it end up that you were no longer in the group?

Well I could feel the mounting pressure of the upcoming performance as we were getting ready for the Magic Mountain show, and Melvin was like, "Ok, get it together young buck. Jump up, let's get it together." And one day, I guess I kept doing- I didn't even know, I thought I was doing everything perfect, I just came from the mic singing a lead in Cloud 9, and I was doing the moves (demonstrates choreography...bop, bop hit, hit...) I still know them (the moves) even now, and Melvin was like, "No! You didn't extend your arms out all the way like his, you're doing it wrong." He demonstrated once, and then he went to demonstrate it again and all of a sudden his knee went out and he grabbed his knee and yelled, "Oh, my knee! Oh my knee!" And I thought it was a joke, and the rest of the of the group was laughing, so I started laughing.

And oh, it was over with after that. It was over, cause you know after a few weeks they had gotten used to me and we would joke and laugh with each other so I felt like one of the guys- one of the family. But I was a younger member just joining the group so I didn't realize I didn't have the liberty to laugh in that moment.

Man, Melvin went off! And he had some choice words for me that day...cussed me out. I was only 20 years old...man I was in tears. I sat down and started crying. Otis was so mad and they were like, "Why did you talk to him like that? He was just laughing like us, we're family now." And Melvin was like, (in his bass voice) "Well he shouldn't've been laughing." After that I was so mad and hurt.

As the rookie, I was designated to answer the phones when we took a break. They were like, "You answer the phones and say, 'The Temptations,' and don't say anything else and whatever they say to you, you just tell us. So I'm like, "Ok." So you know, I was hurt after that. I was so crushed. I called my mother later that night, and I was like, "Momma, he said I look like a dog that was about to...(choice words)." So after that I said, no, I don't want to do this." I called my friend Gregory Matter and I told him that I didn't want to stay in the group because of how Melvin spoke to me, and it was also because of some other things I saw just being in the industry that I wasn't able to deal with, and on top of that being humiliated I was ready to go."

It was surreal because whenever we went somewhere, me being the new member at the time, they didn't want anyone to see me yet. But when people saw me and they asked them who I was, they were like, "Oh he replaced Dennis. He's amazing." From how I styled my hair, to the clothes I wore, you know I wanted to look like them and fit in, so I was dressed nice. It was an amazing experience. Meeting David Ruffin was amazing. Meeting Eddie Kendricks-, amazing! Well I had originally met them through Norman Whitfield before I had auditioned for the group. And Whit was one of their original producers and songwriters.

For a moment I almost kind of regretted it (making the decision to leave the group). I came and told them the next day that I didn't want to be in the group. By then I had also called Norman Whitfield, and he told me that he had been saving me a spot in his group Masterpiece, which was the name of the single he produced for the Temptations, but he created a group with the same name. He was like, "You're the lead singer in Masterpiece. You can leave the Tempts and tell them I give you my blessing. And tell them I don't want to hear nothin' negative, but you just come on back home where you belong."

So I went back home and started writing for Norman Whitfield and the group Masterpiece and wrote the album. But see Norman brought David Ruffin to meet with me and talk to me, and he brought Eddie Kendricks by and that greatly encouraged me. They were all tall and very slender. And I remember meeting David Ruffin, shaking his hand and telling him how much I loved his voice and about how many times I would sing his parts to their songs. Like, "Sunshine blue skies, please go away…" It's funny how I used to shape my voice like Dennis' (Edwards) because I was really just a pure tenor, so the Donny Hathaway stuff was right up my alley. But I shaped my voice to have some edge, and that made it a little rougher.

So I didn't want to go back to California and have the groups be like, "They kicked him out of the Tempts, so I knew to call Gregory Matter and I was like, "Hey, I'm leaving the group, but I'm a let you know they didn't put me out of the group, (but that was my pride and that competitive mentality trying to protect my ego and my image from my peers).

NORMAN WHITFIELD

So how did you meet Norman Whitfield?

Well I was going to work for the LA Times, and the buses were on strike, and I was standing on the corner at the bus stop looking to hitch hike, with my thumb out, and driving around the corner here comes Masterpiece, a group that Norman had put together and adopted. When I saw Masterpiece, I quickly put my thumb down, because I knew them and I didn't want them to see me (trying to hitch hike), because it was early in the morning and they all looked up to me you know? [We would sing in the same groups throughout high school and after graduating].

So they were like, "Hey man what are you doing? Are you singing with The Expectations still?" And I was like, "Naw man, I moved over to the westside." And they said, "Hey, can you come to the audition (for Masterpiece) because we know if you come, you'll make the group, and they'll love you." Michael Foley (one of the group members) was also one of my best friends. So they picked me up and brought me to meet Norman. It was like a 2 to 3 hour wait at the studio, and he finally came in (Norman Whitfield) and I was looking like, ok that really is him. You know, I just wanted to make sure that it actually was him, and it was.

When he met me he said, "Oh so you're tall too huh?" (Because Norman was tall). Then he said, "So do you know any songs? They told me you can sing." I said "Yeah, but I haven't been singing (mainstream) lately-I've been singing in church." I had been in church thick during this time singing with the Stewart family, opening up for them as they opened for the Clark Sisters. I said, "I don't know any popular songs right now because I've been singing only in church for a while now, and I kind of mess around with the piano a little." He said, "Here's the piano, sing something, play something."

So I started on a song I was writing on the piano and I started singing it, and I never had a hook, and I remember him saying, "Wow, you sound great...where's the hook?" I said, "What's that?" He said, "That's the part of the song that repeats itself. The title of the song." Before I could complete my next sentence he said, "You're in. Just come here everyday. Show up everyday. So what do you do?" I said, "Well I work for LA Times but they are on strike." Then he said, "You need money." And I was like, "Yeah."

HOW TO DELIVER A SONG WITH IMPACTFUL EMOTION

And from that point, he just took me in. And I didn't realize how blessed I was until I really researched and observed him, because I knew his name and all those songs he did, but when I was able to spend time with him and just watch how he carried himself...I mean Norman had so much money, so many houses and cars, but when I saw him in the studio, that's what had me in awe. He would allow me to just hang out and watch him produce, and the rest of the group would be off doing their thing, but Norman knew that I wanted to learn, and he could sense that I wanted to be be mentored. So as soon as he told me what a hook was, I said, "Ok, I'll write it." And that was the first song I wrote...which went on Rose Royce, called *Help*. It was really weird to achieve that hook like that.

It was wonderful because I would see all these stars that would come just to say hi to Norman Whitfield and I mean he knew everybody. Everybody would just come there (Norman's studio) because he was just such a great songwriter and producer. He would always say, "Hey this is Rob, my writer and the lead singer in Masterpiece." So right then and there, Masterpiece was looking like, how is he just gonna come and take over? I remember one time I came late to our studio session because my car needed a battery, and that very same day, Norman took me to buy another car.

My thing was with Norman Whitfield, if he said I could come in the studio, I was sitting right there- never said a word. I would sit in the corner and watch everything he did. He noticed that, and he noticed that I was able to handle being around all those stars and just keep a cool vibe. But I mean I would never say a word. And I remember when I started recording *Help* in the studio with Rose Royce- one day it was a big party and everybody was there, Gladys Knight, and he didn't know, but I was still in the studio room where they would record the musicians and they had mic'd the drums and some of the artists and musicians were also in there like Wah Wah Watson and Joe "Pep" Harris (Undisputed

Truth). So I didn't know you could hear on the outside everything going on in that room from the speaker. So the door was closed, and I was just going over a piano part, and Michael Nash and someone else were like, "Hey, so who's your idol? Like who do you idolize yourself after?" And I said, "I don't believe in idols and having an idol. I'm my only idol. I don't believe in that type of stuff."

Norman Whitfield's group, Masterpiece. I am in the top left-hand corner on the back of the album cover (above). There were five of us but one group member missed the photoshoot.

And so Norman and them heard it. And when I came out he was like, "So you don't have an idol huh?" And I was like, "Oh!" You know because (in saying that) I was trying to be like Norman. So when they said, "Who's your idol?" I was like, "What? I don't do that. I don't have an idol." You know that's the first thing I said cause I was with Norman, and the way he carried himself...I wanted to be like that too. Norman would frown up at the idol stuff, so from that moment on, I was like his right hand. So Joe and them were like, "Yeah, you can write." And Miles Gregory and Billie Calvin who wrote, "Wishing On A Star," they all loved me and treated me well. So you know when Norman was like, "You know that piano over there in my other office? It's yours. Just go ahead and write everyday."

I was there day and night...until Billie Calvin or Miles Gregory would come over there, but I was there. Then he told me, "You write the groups album." Because you know, I was getting tired of waiting and I wanted to leave the group because it was taking so long. I had even thought about going to sing for Charlie Wilson's project, but I ended up hanging in there.

I have never to this day seen anyone do what Norman Whitfield did in his time and I mean in his attitude, he just decided he was going to write a hit. And he knew it was a hit and he couldn't even play the piano but would just start banging on the piano and would be like, "Yeah, do it like this! Listen!" Norman was so phenomenal and such a visionary. I watched him change songs and make them hits. See what Norman did was he took sounds, and made music from sounds. He would sonically take music from sounds. I mean whatever the sound was, he would just take it and create music from it.

He was one of the greatest producers that has ever lived. I mean before electronics and drum machines. Norman was an all out producer. That didn't mean that you did a track and stopped there, that meant that you produced and did the music, wrote the lyrics, and produced the vocals, arranged the harmonies, produced results. Babyface is like that. These days producers have teams. I saw all the greats perform from The Four Tops, The Young Hearts, The O'Jays, they would come to this place called The Total Experience (in Los Angeles). Before that I was in a group called The Expectations, and we modeled ourselves after the Tempts. Our group performed opening for The Temptations, The Four Tops, Lakeside, and other acts like that.

Norman was also a pool shark, and he was very good at basketball. I mean he could shoot that rock and handle the ball. But Norman was a hustler. He talked about Motown and being in Detroit around all those groups and about how competitive it was. And it was Whitfield and Strong, and the Jackson's. And he would tell me the different Motown stories and how they would have all theses different rooms with writers in them like Holland-Dozier-Holland and Whitfield and Strong, and Smokey Robinson, and how competitive it was. Norman, he was very competitive, but he was so brilliant. *Which Way Is Up* was a movie he wrote the theme song to and he wrote the infamous theme song to the movie *Car Wash*, and more! Norman was competitive and he could come up with a hit. One thing about Norman is that if it (a song) wasn't a hit, he would be like, "Ok, this ain't happenin', let's move on." He would shut it down. He was a no-nonsense person when it came to creativity. You know he had Eddie Bongo Brown, Wah Wah Watson...the greats. He was looking for great writers. And he brought me in and he noticed that I was more of a pop writer, because *I Wonder Where You Are Tonight* and those songs were more pop, while alot of his main writers were more R&B.
He brought this kid to me as he was going to have me take him under my wing because he also wrote in that pop vein like I did. But I don't know what happened to him because he left before it could materialize. He was from a wealthy and privileged family though. One day he just disappeared and we never saw him again.

HOW TO DELIVER A SONG WITH IMPACTFUL EMOTION

(Circa 1980) Me here with group member, Michael Foley, producing the vocals for the *Masterpiece* album.

ROSE ROYCE

One of the main groups Norman Whitfield had you writing for was Rose Royce.

How did that all start?

Well actually when I began working with them, I wasn't writing my first song for Rose Royce. I was actually writing my first song for Masterpiece, but when Norman heard it, he just took it. He was like, "Hey, I need a record." So I played him my very first song called, *Help*. I told him, "Hey I have a song for us (Masterpiece) and he said, "Let me hear it." And I played it for him. And he said, "Yep, that's Rose Royce, they're going to record it." So my first record, my first song that I ever wrote, was called, *Help,* and it was recorded by Rose Royce. I would see Rose Royce everyday and our groups were competitive with one another.

My group Masterpiece sang on the hit Car Wash, even though I didn't sing with them on it, they got paid and were feeling some type of way because they were ready to be next and the hits were going to Rose Royce. But they knew it wasn't out time yet. We all worked together all the time. Many people didn't know this, but when Undisputed Truth left Motown, Rose Royce who backed them as musicians, wore disguises and head pieces over their faces to conceal their identity at the time. I was told they even wore paper bags over their heads. My friend, who played with Rose Royce told me that.

Norman put Rose Royce together initially because of the lead singer Gwen. And once Norman left Motown and started his own label, Whitfield Records, he saved a spot for me in the group, Masterpiece, and that's when he told me to come back home when I was with the Temptations. Rose Royce played for us and we sang for them.

What were the sessions like working with Rose Royce? You did a quite a few songs with them. (*I Wonder Where You Are Tonight, Shine Your Light, Best Love, Help, And You Wish For Yesterday, and Tell Me That I'm Dreaming*)

They were great! I used to sit in the booth with Norman while he was producing them (Rose Royce). So I saw him produce vocals. I mean he said he could get a hit off of a chicken! (Chuckles) I mean he was like, "All you have to do is show up." That's how incredible Norman was. Norman Whitfield's thing was to get the emotion out of you on a record. That's what he taught me, being in Masterpiece, how to capture emotion. He used to say, "Squeeze the Charmin's" and that means give me everything you got! I felt sorry for the engineers though, because if you missed something, or didn't catch it, or erased it...he went off! Norman had two engineers working at the same time when it was a huge project. They rotated usually.

I would be in at almost every session every opportunity I got. Norman would always start with the drums. He would spend time microphoning every drum. I remember how he would get that beat...and I didn't realize how serious it was to record a session to where you had to record and mic the drums to get the perfect sound, and of course you had to mic the piano. He would do that and bring in the rhythm section featuring Jack Ashford, and would have those musicians Michael Nash and Dean Gant, and others in the session and record all the music first. Then he would have the group, which in this case was Rose Royce come in and record the vocals. But before he brought the group in, he would take the lead singer in the studio first, because he wanted to capture all the emotion from the lead vocalist for the song and that would set the table for the rest of the group and background vocalists. He would spend a significant amount of time just capturing emotions.

So how would you compare this formula with today's process of recording?

Well, it's technology now. Sometimes you may add the background vocals in after a lead has been laid to give the vocalist some support and something to bounce off of. But with Norman when it came to vocals, he got everything out of that lead vocalist. And if you didn't write the song you were singing, he would have you study it. Like when Gwen (Dickey) would sing one of my songs he would have me record it first, and then have her study it, and study the emotion of it before she laid her vocal. You had to study the song so before you came into the studio, you knew what you were doing and you were ready to go.

In the recording process Norman did all the musical production and the vocal production. He allowed me to be in the studio by myself with our group because he understood that I studied him and knew what he expected. Now of course he would come in and fix what needed to be fixed. If I had to sing something over he would have me do it. But Norman would bring stuff out of me that I didn't even know was in me. I mean he produced the Tempts, Gladys, Smokey.

So again, this was very different from today's process.

Well yeah. Today you can record 20 tracks of the lead vocal and then come back and vocal comp it. But back in that day, you just had to sing, and you wouldn't have but a couple of tracks. If you didn't get it right, then he would take a break and then come back when you had it. It wasn't a bunch of tracks. You had that one more track to nail it.

Then from knowing Norman Whitfield I was introduced to Leon Sylvers and I would go to Shalamar's sessions with him.

THE FOUR TOPS

What was it like working with The Four Tops, especially after getting an opportunity to be a member of The Temptations?

It was an amazing and classic experience. You know, The Four Tops have just about as many hits as the Temptations actually. And then they had The Four Tops and Temptations review. It was incredible to see them go back and forth with their hits.

What was the Four Tops' work ethic like?

They were the consummate professionals. They would all be there and then waited for Levi to make his entrance. I really worked with Levi mostly because when we were in the studio, the group would be waiting for Levi to come in and record his lead vocals before they would record their background vocals. And when Levi came in like an hour later, you would see how amazing he was. He had so much raw ability with a big raspy voice. He made sure he really laid the vocal down fully. I was there as a writer and I would just make sure they got the verses down, but I didn't spend much time with them outside of that. They were a very private group. They were straight to business because they knew they were stars so they didn't spend much time with that other stuff (socializing with everyone outside of working).

LAKESIDE

When did you start working with Lakeside?

It was after they changed labels and after their Fantastic Voyage album. I worked on their album *Party Patrol*. But at the time, I was writing music for my solo album. So the songs *Sailing*, *Money*, and

Think Twice were actually intended for my album. I was about to go to Columbia Records, Warner Bros, or Motown. I ended up at Epic for a moment. I worked with Lakeside through Norman Whitfield and then Dennis Nelson, and that's how I met Thomas Dawson (of the Commodores). During this time I also met Dick Griffey who introduced me to Dina Andrews from Solar Records.

Babyface had just split from LA Reid and Dick Griffey was looking to find another writing and production team with myself and Dennis Nelson, but I didn't end up signing the production contract. Dennis had a song called *Money* that was already produced and I finished writing it. Although I didn't sign, I stayed to make sure the records were cut and I vocally produced Lakeside. When it came to working with Lakeside, we had a history and our groups were always competitive with one another in singing and they had that big hit so... it was a lot of egos in the room.

DR. DRE

How did you end up signing to Aftermath with Dr. Dre?

It was through Bradley Spalter, whom I met through Emanuel Officer, whom I met through my sister Meni. I think...it's hard to remember who I met Emanuel through. This was around the late 90's and I was working on my solo album. Dre heard some of my music. I was actually about to sign with Warner Bros through Maani Edwards. I was a writer at EMI at the time and I went over to Universal Music Publishing to record over there where Maani was.

When Dre heard my music he met me and wanted to sign me. But I told him, "Hey, I have a group I am in now." So he said, "Ok, I'll sign the group to get you." So he signed the group as ESP. I'll never forget when I met Dr. Dre one-on-one right after he left

Death Row and started Aftermath, he said "Can you fight?" "I said, 'Can I fight? I mean yeah if I have to. Yeah'." So we began the group.

We would all be in the studio and Dr. Dre would be like, "Come on Storm..." and I would get in the limo with him and then my group and the other guys at the label wasn't feeling that either. Me and Dre were always cool and appreciated each other and he knew I worked with Norman Whitfield and everything. David Ruffin's son was also at Aftermath at the time and me just coming on board and having a little favoritism caused some tension there.

How did you end up transitioning out of Aftermath?

There was too much tension. Every time we turned around Dre was like, "Storm, what happened now?" So I was like, you gotta let me outta my contract. And he let me out of my contract, and dropped the group. My group was mad but hey...things were getting outta hand. I was a different person then, but the environment was volatile. Not too many people liked me there except for a couple of the producers and musicians.

(Above) Here I am (center) with my group ESP during a photoshoot during the time we were signed to Dr. Dre's Aftermath. (Below) Me hanging out (center) with the group and some affiliates before we got into our limos to our next destination.

ROBIN THICKE

How did you meet Robin Thicke?

Well I was looking for a manager at the time, because I had just fired my manager the same day I found out he signed Brian McKnight. We had different types of music, but our sound was too similar at the time. That was too close for comfort for me at the time, and Brian and I had a couple run-ins on the basketball court previously so (at that time) I didn't like him that much. I mean I'd be getting fouled hard and the other players wouldn't even tap him (Brian McKnight) on the wrist, and I'd be like, "Hey, how come ya'll not foulin' him?" and they would be like, "Come on man that's Brian McKnight." (Chuckling) Yes I know I had an ego, and was a little bitter about that whole management thing, but they were beating me at the (basketball) hole...and this is before I rededicated my life back to Christ so of course I would have handled the situation differently then, but I truly believe it all worked out. Brian I got nothing but the love of Jesus for you man.

Only God knows where I would have been if I had taken off as an artist at that time. I would've been a train wreck waiting to happen finally having to deal with all that pressure and limelight an artist deals with. I had been running for a long time with failed marriages and strained relationships with my children, but music was therapy for me all those years and still is a form of therapy. But now that I have Jesus, God's word...it's amazing!

But anyway, like I said, I was looking for another manager and I called my friend Stacey Lieb, and she told me to contact Miguel Melendez, who was working with Will Smith. So they set up a meeting and I met him at EMI and he listened to my music and was like, "Man, you kind of sound like my artist, Robin Thicke, he's 16. Can I have him come and meet you?" That's when EMI was on Sunset before they moved to Santa Monica. So the next day, they had brought Robin to meet me, and I was like, "Hey, wassup?" He (Robin) said, "Hey you're Storm?" I said, "Yeah, I'm Storm" and he said, "Why are you Storm?" and I said, "I'm just Storm-that's it." And he was like, "Why?" And I'm like, "That's the reason why?" (Chuckles).

Yeah, I didn't know who he was but then he was like, "Can you come over to my house and we can work?" They were looking for him to work with someone because he had working with Brian McKnight but I guess that situation didn't pan out. So then I went to his house the next day. And from that day on, it was history. I heard him sing and I was like, "Wait a minute!" Robin was so ahead of his time because he could write, and sing, and play the piano. He is seriously a true songwriter. We sounded similar in some areas at times, but I was raspier and he was coming into his own. Our melodies complemented each other and we just had this chemistry going like the infamous songwriting duos. From that point we were working together like everyday and began to make history.

Any unforgettable moments you can remember working with Robin?

I remember when we were writing Shooter, he had already started on the song, and I had gone driving around trying to buy some clothes or something. Robin and ProJay were already in the studio. So then Robin called me and was like, "Hey! Come to the studio..." So of course I dropped everything I was doing and I came up there, and at this point, I had developed a certain thing that I do called, Freestyle Melody Writing. He told me a story about how that as a kid, he was inside of a bank during an actual bank robbery, and how they told everyone to get down on the floor.

So I was like, "Don't play me nothin' (previously recorded). Just play the track and put me on the mic. Just record me and let me go." He was like, "Yeah ok, go ahead and get on the mic." So as I heard the music, I was like, "I- heard- some shots- like- down on the flo—-or…" And at that moment, he started running around the house and jumping up and down and started celebrating. And that was how Shooter came about. It was a spastic approach. Robin had the hook and I came with the verses. I would've been up there later anyway, but that creative moment was like, "right now."

A Word for the Inside…

Ecclesiastes 3: 9-15

9 What profit has the worker from that in which he labors? **10** I have seen the God-given task with which the sons of men are to be occupied. **11** He has made everything beautiful in its time. Also He has put eternity in their hearts, except that no one can find out the work that God does from beginning to end.

12 I know that nothing is better for them than to rejoice, and to do good in their lives, **13** and also that every man should eat and drink and enjoy the good of all his labor—it is the gift of God.
14 I know that whatever God does,
It shall be forever.
Nothing can be added to it,
And nothing taken from it.
God does it, that men should fear before Him.

15 That which is has already been,
And what is to be has already been;
And God requires an account of what is past.

Romans 8:28
28 And we know that all things work together for good to those who love God, to those who are the called according to His purpose.

1 Corinthians 7:17-20

17 But as God has distributed to each one, as the Lord has called each one, so let him walk. And so I ordain in all the churches. **18** Was anyone called while circumcised? Let him not become uncircumcised. Was anyone called while uncircumcised? Let him not be circumcised. **19** Circumcision is nothing and uncircumcision is nothing, but keeping the commandments of God is what matters. **20** Let each one remain in the same calling in which he was called. **21** Were you called while a slave? Do not be concerned about it; but if you can be made free, rather use it. **22** For he who is called in the Lord while a slave is the Lord's freedman. Likewise he who is called while free is Christ's slave. **23** You were bought at a price; do not become slaves of men. **24** Brethren, let each one remain with God in that state in which he was called.

Colossians 3:23-25

23 And whatever you do, do it heartily, as to the Lord and not to men, **24** knowing that from the Lord you will receive the reward of the inheritance; for you serve the Lord Christ. **25** But he who does wrong will be repaid for what he has done, and there is no partiality.

MAY GOD BLESS THE READER AND THE
HEARER OF HIS WORD IN JESUS NAME

Thank you for taking a moment to share in my testimony and gift.

I pray you are touched in some way that has impacted you for impacting others.

Pictured Above: (L to R) Pastor Frank Starks III, Pastor Kenneth Mulkey, myself, and my beautiful wife Rosetta at my graduation ceremony from Cottonwood Ministry College. (Below) Visiting as a special guest of World Harvest Church in Columbus, OH with Pastor Rod Parsley, congregation and friends.

A Special Thank You to Our Partner and The Contributor for Our Audio Version of this Book

"HOW TO DELIVER A SONG WITH IMPACTFUL EMOTION"

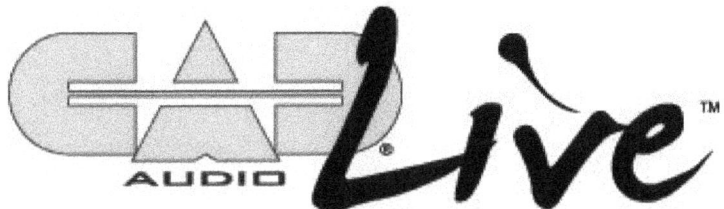

References

The Holy Bible (King James Version)

ABOUT THE AUTHOR

An ordained and licensed minister of the gospel of Jesus Christ, Robert "Elijah Storm" Daniels, is blessed to enjoy his longtime profession as a Grammy Award winning songwriter, producer, vocal coach, author, and public speaker, with Billboard chart success spanning over 40 years. A Los Angeles native, Robert Louis Daniels, p.k.a Elijah Storm, is a close descendant of the infamous Ohio native quartet group, The Mills Brothers, and began his career as a protege of the legendary Norman Whitfield (Motown) in the 1970's, spending a brief stint with the group The Temptations, and being featured in Whitfield's group Masterpiece (The Girl's Alright With Me) before writing for such groups as Rose Royce, Willie Hutch, and Lakeside. Elijah Storm is most recognized in the music industry for his collaborations with Robin Thicke (Evolution of Robin Thicke), and Usher (Confessions). Classically trained with a background in gospel, Elijah Storm is sought after for his signature style of vocal arrangements, freestyle melody writing, and hair-raising harmonic blends. Paralleling his musical gifts is his gift of imparting confidence and bringing out the best in the artists he works with, which sets him apart in the harsh world of the music business. Author of his upcoming book release, How To Deliver A Song With Impactful Emotion A Ministers 40 Year Collection of Winning Recipes to Revolutionize Your Singing Experience, Elijah Storm's book tour will demonstrate to his audience life-changing techniques to enhance their gifts. When working with his clients, Elijah Storm provides a combination of services including vocal training &

coaching, vocal production, and artist development, as well as mentors a portion of his students with valuable wisdom in using their gifts for the purpose in which they were created. His technique and approach produces real results which are measurable in a short time. Elijah Storm's lyrical contribution, vocal production and delivery evokes impactful emotion and imagery allowing his music to influence millions worldwide. He is the CEO of BIGG KIDD MUSIC, the music director, Associate Pastor, and board member of Exciting Ministries, a 501 (c)(3) non-profit outreach ministry, and Director of S.T.A.R.S. Cleveland, a non-profit program for teen development. Storm recently relocated from Los Angeles to Cleveland to labor in his assignment the Lord called him to back in 2008 when he first ministered at World Harvest Church in Columbus, OH, ministering to underprivileged youth and young adults.

Over the years he has spoken to youth as a guest speaker through various organizations including the Grammy Museum, Cottonwood Leadership College, World Harvest Church, the YMCA, and has served the Long Beach Action Community Partnership organization as an instructor through the L.A.M.P. (Leadership Academy Mentoring Program). He has taught music fundamentals and vocals at Ramah Junior Academy in Cleveland, OH and continues to partner with his community through workshops imparting into youth and young adults Christian principles, wisdom from his own testimony in the music business, and artist development training with life skills. Currently residing in Cleveland Heights, OH, with his wife and children, Elijah Storm's clientele includes all ages throughout the world.

WORKSHOPS & BOOK TOURS

HOW TO DELIVER A SONG WITH IMPACTFUL EMOTION
This session includes personal vocal coaching and training that covers singing fundamentals, executing confidence, power, and control, song interpretation and delivery, finding your unique tone and much more!

VOCAL THERAPY...THE SOUND OF HEALING
This session includes crucial breathing techniques, defining tone, protecting and strengthening your vocal chords, developing a listening ear, and more!

GOD'S ANOINTED VESSEL: SUPERNATURAL VOCAL EMPOWERMENT
This session includes revelation of vocal instrumentation, impartation of vocal techniques for skill enhancement, and vocal empowerment in praise and worship for God's glory in Christ Jesus.

Host a speaking engagement, workshop or class session!

WORSHIP. EDUCATION. WELLNESS. RECREATION.

Visit:

www.SupernaturalVocals.com

BIGG KIDD MUSIC

Robert "Elijah Storm" Daniels

3 Severance Circle #181130

Cleveland, OH 44118

440-941-1779

supernaturalvocals@gmail.com

Products also available from:

BIGG KIDD MUSIC

VIRTUAL VOCAL LESSONS
enable you to receive in the comfort of your own home, interactive, custom training and tools that will perfect your unique sound! Learn singing fundamentals, voice strengthening, song interpretation and delivery, and much more!

"HOW TO DELIVER A SONG WITH IMPACTFUL EMOTION"

The E-book

"HOW TO DELIVER A SONG WITH IMPACTFUL EMOTION"

The Audio Book

FREEDOM

The EP by Elijah Storm and Rhema Rose

Visit our website for updates and more!

www.SupernaturalVocals.com

www.ingramcontent.com/pod-product-compliance
Lightning Source LLC
Chambersburg PA
CBHW070051120426
42742CB00048B/2400